SCALE in ARCHITECTURE

SCALE im ARCHITECTURE

Frank Orr

VAN NOSTRAND REINHOLD COMPANY
NEW YORK

Copyright (c) 1985 by Van Nostrand Reinhold Company Inc.
Library of Congress Catalog Card Number 84–20886
ISBN 0–442–27245–6 paper

Printed in the United States of America
Designed by Ernie Haim

Published by Van Nostrand Reinhold Company Inc.
115 Fifth Avenue
New York, New York 10003

Van Nostrand Reinhold Company Limited
Molly Millars Lane
Wokingham, Berkshire RG11 2PY, England

Van Nostrand Reinhold
480 La Trobe Street
Melbourne, Victoria 3000, Australia

Macmillan of Canada
Division of Canada Publishing Corporation
164 Commander Boulevard
Agincourt, Ontario M1S 3C7, Canada

16   15   14   13   12   11   10   9   8   7   6   5   4   3   2

Library of Congress Cataloging in Publication Data

Orr, Frank, 1932—
    Scale in architecture.

    Includes index.
    1. Architecture—Composition, proportion, etc.
I. Title.
NA2760.076   1985   720′.1   84–20886
ISBN 0–442–27245–6 (pbk.)

To all architects, from Senmut forward—including all those who will grace the world in future days—and especially to Vitruvius: no one has yet defined the proper aims of architecture better than with the words "firmness, commodity, and delight."

Contents

Acknowledgments

Some of the people who helped shape my views on architectural scale—either through personal contact or through the legacy of their contributions to our craft—are specifically mentioned in the text.

Among those who are not mentioned elsewhere are three teachers I had the privilege of studying under at Auburn University: Edward Marty, who explained the mysteries of architectural history to me with such love and clarity; Stan Thomasson, who constantly asked the right questions; and Ralph Knowles, who introduced me to the concept of a "range-of-scale" and who later gained a well-deserved reputation in energy-conscious design research, writing, and education.

The late Edwin A. Keeble taught me more about scale—and many other facets of architecture—than all my other teachers combined. It was my privilege and (more often than not) pleasure to serve an 8-year apprenticeship under him.

There are many other people who assisted in a variety of ways: Steven A. Kliment, chairman of the AIA Environmental Education Committee during the first part of my service on that committee, who has been so generous with advice and counsel; Milton Graves of the Auburn University physical plant department; Carl Manka of the Tennessee State Architect's office; Everett Henry of the Metropolitan

Nashville Department of Education; Charles May of Nashville State Technical Institute; and Nashville architects Terrill Hall and Don Miller.

An expression of gratitude of a special sort is due Steven Gray, my editor. He socratically cajoled, cheered, coached, charmed, and shamed me into making the same kind of effort toward quality in writing that I have tried in this book to urge the architectural community to make toward excellence in architecture.

Finally, my dear wife, Nancy, and my equally long-suffering partner, Ed Houk, deserve my special thanks.

1. Introduction

When I first entered college, soon after the conclusion of World War II, the reigning philosophy in most architectural schools was unashamedly, emphatically *Modern*. Figure 1–1 shows a product of this philosophy—an elementary school dating from the late 1930s.

At the same time, the architectural profession still included many practitioners who had been educated at a time when more traditional ideas were espoused, and these architects continued to design in a vocabulary of traditional or historical forms. Some were

1–1. Burton School, Nashville.

attempting a personal transition, but they did not fully reject the past as the Modern masters decreed. The simplified Doric forms shown in figure 1–2 are illustrative of the evolution from traditional architectural design to Modernism that occurred in the middle third of this century: the effects of Modernism may be seen most prominently in the entablature and pediment, which have been wiped absolutely clean of ornament; the surface is relieved only by a very simple, Modern round louver.

Generally, for those educated in my generation and in most generations since, the exposure to architectural history has been minimal. Moreover, the history that is studied is often approached with the wrong objective in mind: merely to enable an architect to recognize certain buildings and historical periods. Too seldom were and are the questions explored of *why* a civilization built the way it did and *what* application of those reasons can be profitably made to our current time and civilization.

Just as some great technological achievements, such as the development of concrete, had to be recreated when the original knowledge was lost to mankind, some valuable threads of the fabric of architecture now being lost because of the progressive devaluation of history as a resource for architectural discipline and invention may only be relearned in the future through slow and painful experience.

A few years ago, some architects began questing for a richer kind of architecture than Modernism seemed able to produce. A major resource in this search was the past. At first, the movement was referred to as "historical allusionism" or "historical reference," and later it came to be known as "post-Modernism"—although the movement that inspired these terms was committed to much more than the idea of mining the lodes of the past for design inspiration.

The private residence shown in figure 1–3 illustrates two prominent ideas of post-Modernism:

1–2. Vine Street Christian Church, Nashville.

1–3. Private residence, Franklin, Tennessee.

1–4. Office building, Nashville.

1–5. Claridge Condominiums, Nashville.

clear reference to traditional forms, without slavish copying; and (in the "peeling away" of the front wall on the left) the superimposition of Modern planning principles onto what we would have expected to be a traditional floor plan.

Two other examples of recent building based on traditional form are shown in figures 1–4 and 1–5. The former shows a rather close adherence to Palladian ideas, filtered through an interpretation of the Georgian period; the latter is a somewhat freer specimen, using Georgian motifs hung on the armature of Modern apartment forms.

The important questions to ask about post-Modernism are: why was it felt necessary to look beyond the capacities of Modernism, and what constitute appropriate responses to this perceived need?

Many writers have focused on perceived deficiences of Modernism—its rigidity, moralistic tone, austerity, faulty sociological assumptions, and lack of concern—for a range of human emotional needs. My intention, at least in part, is to add to and expand upon the valid ideas and observations of these writers by focusing on scale—an essential element of design that may already have been damaged by the effects of the Modern purging of history so severely as to approximate the technological loss of concrete during the Dark Ages. I further hope to demonstrate that this loss is a leading cause of the current, widely experienced disenchantment with Modern architecture.

What else can explain, in the face of the commercial and industrial world's overwhelming commitment to the Modern idiom—manifested, for example, in the small office building shown in figure 1–6—the continuing allegiance to traditional forms that is demonstrated in private residences and to a lesser degree in religious, hospitality, and academic architecture?*

Although the buyers of such structures may be represented at the emotional end of a scale whose opposite end terminates at untempered rationalism, they may also be seen as the only purchasers on the architectural market for whom deep-felt emotional needs bear at least equal weight with functional economy— for whom economic return is not the principal criterion for decisions. Indeed, nonarchitects, in the wisdom of their common sense, may have understood all along that they needed the visual enrichment provided

by the scale-giving elements found in the classical orders and in other devalued traditions in architecture.

Whatever the reasons for public rejection of the tenets and products of Modern architecture, the question is not how can people be made to see that Modernism is good and deserves to be embraced? The question is, are there lessons to be learned from this observed phenomenon and, if so, what are they and how can we—the public as well as the architectural profession—benefit from them? Although this compound question is a difficult one to answer, the response I develop over the course of this book involves reintroducing scale to the architectural profession and to the sensitive public.

Two examples from my personal experience may strike similar chords of resonance in the reader.

One very meaningful period of my life was the four years I served on the American Institute of Architects' Committee on Environmental Education. Most of the meetings were held in Washington; and while I had visited Washington previously, my visits had always been brief. Being there for the meetings gave me opportunity to see not only the well-known and revered public monuments but also a great many banal office buildings, cloaked in gray-beige uniforms of stone and precast concrete, just as thousands of government workers seemed to be dressed in the gray uniform of three-piece business suits.

On one visit I was the house guest of a college friend who was a bureaucrat and not an architect. The Kennedy Center for the Performing Arts had just been completed and my friend asked me what I thought of it. I replied that I had not seen it at close enough hand

* A renewed interest in or continued adherence to historical forms can be seen in other areas of American and Western culture. In popular painting, sculpture, drama, music, and even in poetry, the market has never been better for the realistic and the traditional. Consider, for example, the resurgent popularity of wildlife prints, antique collecting (and reproduction), country and gospel music, and mountain crafts.

1—6. Braswell Building, Nashville.

to make a serious judgment, but that at the distance at which I *had* viewed it, it seemed to suffer from being "out of scale." He concurred, although neither of us could define what "out of scale" meant. As I later pondered this question, I decided that a serious and comprehensive definition of scale was badly needed.

At a later meeting of the same AIA committee in St. Louis, I found a surprising example of a building that was "in scale." The site of the meeting was a medium-rise, orange-spandreled, curtain-walled, cylindrical motel decorated and furnished in garish "Motel Mediterranean" style.

A few hours before the opening session was to

begin, I met Patrick Quinn, FAIA, the witty and erudite then-chairman of the School of Architecture at Rensselaer Polytechnic Institute, and we decided to take a stroll around the neighborhood. The motel was located at one of the corners formed by the intersection of two monstrous, multilane, unlimited-access arterials. On one of the other three corners stood an automobile dealership; on another, some vaguely industrial-looking buildings; and on the last, a large, undistinguished apartment complex.

The apartments seemed to us to be the most promising architecturally, so we approached them. As we did so, we saw to our surprise and delight that hidden in a little walled enclosure and huddled up next to the apartments was a small but beautifully scaled church. I remember that it was there to serve a deaf congregation, which perhaps partly explains why it had succeeded so well in visual terms. Both Patrick and I were enchanted and exclaimed to each other about what "good scale" it had.

As a student and as a practitioner, I have always believed that there is quite a bit more to scale than most architects and books I encountered ever expressed. I believe that the best designers throughout history have had an intuitive understanding of how to use scale effectively, and that in the formative years of the profession designers had the opportunity to learn the fundamentals of scale by word of mouth through the apprenticeship method of education. I suspect that architects trained in the Beaux Arts tradition were exposed to these fundamentals as well, but were not made to master them, for which reason they were lost, just as knowledge of concrete and of passive-energy-conscious design were lost for so long.

I hope this book will contribute to the rediscovery of these fundamentals—not just awareness of good or poor scale, but also knowledge of why and how scale works. My aim is to encourage architects to become more sensitive to the value of scale, to point out the effects it has on the viewing and using public, and to underscore the present (and future) need for architects to develop the art of establishing appropriate and appealing scale in their buildings.

2. Definitions

"**Scale**" **is a word** that is used rather indiscriminately in conversation and applied to a wide range of notions. In origin, it relates to measurement, as is shown by one of its definitions: the measuring instrument that architects, engineers, and other designers use in making proportionate drawings that differ in size but not in basic form from the physical things they represent. Indeed, it has been difficult to write this last statement without using the word "scale" in another sense—to indicate a change from one physical size to another.

"Scale" also has an application in music that, while derived for recognizable reasons from the same Latin root as the architectural concept, has little direct correlation with the visual properties of scale. See figure 2–1.

The Latin word *scala* meant a ladder or a flight of stairs. In more modern application, scale came to signify a series of marks made at regular intervals

2–1. C-major music scale.

along a line, and later a device or system for measuring. The musical application relates more directly to the idea of ascending steps. See figure 2–2. But there is no satisfactory definition of the architectural application in most general-use dictionaries.

Most definitions of architectural scale developed by writers on the subject are based on the notion of the size of something—a building, a room, a part of a

2–2. Main stair, Tennessee State Capitol, Nashville.

building or room—as it relates to something else. The something else may be physical or it may be an idea, such as our expectation of what the appropriate size of the object should be.

I recently tried to discover some consensus on the definition of scale in five recent books on architecture (the earliest of which was written in 1959) that addressed the task. My investigation yielded eleven identifiable concepts (figure 2–3), only two of which appeared in all five books: the general notion of comparison or relation in size to something else, and the specific comparison or relation to human size. Three authors mentioned the relation to other parts of the same whole, and the relation to the "usual" size of an object; and two dwelt at some length on proportion and proportional theory.

If identifying the nature and extent of our concept of scale is a difficult task in which few points of unanimity appear, we nonetheless agree that the idea of scale offers a means of approaching a basic and important feeling about the way a thing fits together—with itself, with its environment, and with those who view it. There remains the need to give expression to the underlying definition of scale in an operable form.

What I believe is operable is the test of "fitness"; the larger issue to be addressed is not how things relate but how they "fit," both as individual parts and as a completed whole. The creation or design of the architectural relationships ultimately produced may well have been primarily intuitive in past history, but I also believe it is possible to teach or otherwise prepare a person (including oneself) to be more sensitive to the possibilities scale offers in a given situation and to become more competent in expressing them.

If we recognize the scale of a building, even on an intuitive or subconscious level, our feelings of security and well-being are reinforced. We know where we fit in that scale: we have our moorings. This being so, we are comforted and made to feel at ease by our sense of the building's "fitness," which leads to pleasant associations with the building and to our liking and enjoying it.

"Fitness" conveys the idea of balance, of harmony, of dynamic symmetry, of honest expression of the size of structural elements and, in general, of a pleasing and satisfying wholeness, such as we often are able to recognize in other arts.

"Fitness" of scale should be one of the primary goals of design in architecture, even though it largely must be judged on a highly personal and subjective level. To a certain extent, buildings whose "fitness" has been consistently accepted by others—not only among architects, but also by the general public—can serve us as models. Ultimately, however, the sensitive and competent designer must accept and try to fulfill the goal of instilling in every creation a personally meaningful quality and expression of "fitness."

I offer the following as a working definition of architectural scale:

Scale is the aspect in architecture that makes buildings intelligible to us: it gives us a sense of how to relate to the building, and it does so in a way that either attracts us and reinforces our values or repels us and contradicts our values.*

* Of course, scale can show us alternatives to our values and can move us to extend those we now have, but each of us must exercise personal judgment about these values and must choose, on the basis of the best information available and our own wisdom, what they will be and how they will be expressed.

CONCEPT	BOOK				
	A	B	C	D	E
COMPARISON	X	X	X	X	X
RELATED TO WHOLE		X	X		
RELATED TO PARTS		X	X		X
RELATED TO USUAL SIZE			X	X	X
RELATED TO HUMAN SIZE	X	X	X	X	X
PROPORTIONAL THEORY	X				X
MUSICAL ANALOGY	X				
BALANCE		X			
STRENGTH OF MATERIALS		X			
PSYCHOLOGICAL				X	
PERCEPTION					X

LEGEND

A Steen Eiler Rasmussen, *Experiencing Architecture* (Cambridge: M.I.T. Press, 1959).

B Forrest Wilson, *Architecture: A Book of Projects for Young Adults* (New York: Van Nostrand Reinhold, 1968).

C Charles Moore and Gerald Allen, *Dimensions* (New York: Architectural Record Books, 1976).

D Caudill, Pena, and Kennon, *Architecture and You* (New York: Whitney Library of Design, 1978).

E Francis D. K. Ching, *Architecture: Form, Space, and Order* (New York: Van Nostrand Reinhold, 1979).

2–3. Comparison of concepts of scale found in five books.

Good scale in architecture, then, may be said to describe a relationship of visual and textural elements to the whole, to each other, and to the human participant/observer that has been planned and arranged to contribute as fully as possible to the participant/observer's sense of visual satisfaction in the wholeness and fitness of the constructed design.

Understanding scale in architecture begins with understanding the variables and principles affecting scale, as well as their applications in real life settings. Good scale is achieved when personal insight and the wisdom of the ages are integrated into the design process to produce wholeness, beauty, pleasing visual experience, and satisfaction in using the creation so designed.

Because it is almost wholly visual, scale defies more precise definition. Even though its etymological roots definitely involve linearity, it is essentially nonlinear. Instead, it operates in a three-dimensional visual field, with all aspects or components in the field working together to produce the desired result. If the design of a building handles scale well, we will perceive the building as a *gestalt*—a structure whose totality is greater than the sum of its parts—because the functions of scale operate in simultaneously supportive ways.

The ways by which scale is achieved are the subject of the remaining chapters of this book. (One basic premise of the book is that scale in itself is good; *bad* scale would simply be manifested "unfitness"—the absence of the qualities to be investigated here—and *poor* scale would describe a condition in which relatively few of the qualities are present in useful force.)

The purpose of definitions is to give us—author and reader—a comprehensible, coincident starting point. Definitions are *not* the end objective of the book; we get ourselves in trouble when we try to be too exacting and literal-minded in matters having a philosophic and/or aesthetic component. Perhaps at the conclusion of this book, everyone will be able to articulate a more personal definition of scale, which not only expresses a unique vision but also speaks to the broader public.

I will be using a few other terms that are also subject to a wide range of definition. For the sake of clarity, I will state here the meaning I have in mind when using them.

ELEMENT has a generalized, abstract meaning as well as a specific physical meaning. In the study of design, this term can be used abstractly as a collective word for several other, more explicit notions, such as form, line, color, texture, and pattern. The physical application, in architecture, is to such things as doors, windows, walls, and roofs.

FORM means shape or configuration. It can be applied to the entirety of a building, or even to an assemblage of buildings, as well as to a building's parts.

FORMAL means having to do with form, as opposed to having to do with nature or content.

MODERNISM in architecture can signify both the style bearing that name and the architectural theory formulated and promulgated by its proponents. As used here, "Modernism" refers to a general philosophy of design as expressed in architecture, while "Modern architecture" refers to the product of that philosophy. For most architects educated under its tenets, it refers neither to a style nor to a body of dogma but to a way of looking at architectural tasks and at the world at large. In the hands of its best practitioners, it is more accurately defined as a process of analysis and design than as a style.

POST-MODERNISM in architecture refers to architectural design that has moved beyond Modern design in one way or another. It has been used as a cover by people seeking to reintroduce fragments of historical form into current design—often in jarring or discordant juxtapositions—and it has also been applied to recent buildings of wit, charm, and lasting value that (in my view) are simply sequential steps in the long and noble procession of architectural design.

PROPORTION means the relative size of two or more, more-or-less opposing dimensions that are visible at one time.

SIZE refers obviously to physical, measurable dimension. It *may* be understood to imply mass, but usually refers only to dimensions that can be visually determined.

SPACE means the volumetric, three-dimensional void that is visually and/or physically contained by construction. It can be the void within a single room, in an assemblage of linked rooms, or even outdoors— where it refers to the open areas identifiable between and around buildings. All kinds of elements help define space, and they need not all be so obvious as those set at right angles to the horizontal such as walls, screens, and fences; for example, space has a clearly perceived "edge" along planes defined by an abrupt drop-off, as with a cliff, stage front, or similar escarpment.

STYLE is an ambiguous word I prefer not to use. At bottom, it refers to a cluster of formal devices that are found repeatedly in a significant number of buildings from a single historical period and that came to be considered characteristic of the architecture of that period. The danger in using this word is that it can become a dismissive word that cuts off our critical mental processes before we have made the effort necessary for full understanding of the nature and spirit of any particular historical period.

In addition to the preceding, several other terms are defined in the text as it unfolds. For the most part they are words to which I have attached a special meaning for the purpose of discussing the topic of scale.

3. Sources of Scale

The sources of scale in architecture exist in essentially only three forms: in the inherent scale-giving qualities of the materials we use, in the natural world, and in the human body. I have chosen the word "source" to identify the most fundamental lodes from which scale in architecture can be mined. Good scale recognizes, acknowledges, and builds upon these sources.

Many scale-giving characteristics of materials are observable. One involves the nature of the material as it comes to the site ready to be assembled into the building: what are the sizes of the units in which the material arrives at the site? what changes can be made in these units as they are assembled (cut into lengths, bent, or otherwise transformed)? what dimensional range is "natural" to the material?

When we think of such common materials as wood (lumber, in standardized sizes), brick, concrete block, and roof shingles, we immediately have a mental image of the "natural" size of each material, and of its color and texture, even though these can be modified to some degree. The size of a brick is based on what a person can comfortably pick up and put in place with one hand while holding a trowel and applying mortar with the other. Brick transfers its scale-giving nature to everything seen in its context. The scale of the cross and the altar in figure 3–1 and of the stone quoins in figure 3–2 is in each case definitely

3–1. First Christian Church, Glasgow, Kentucky.

established by reference to the universal brick. Similarly, the size of a concrete block is to some extent based on what a person can lift and put in place with two hands.

Stone, too, has its own set of natural scale-giving characteristics. The use of stone as a veneer in the building shown in figure 3–3 communicates in much the same manner as does brick, but at a different amplitude. An entirely different technique, using stones very similar in size, is illustrated in the rock or "slave" fence (figure 3–4) common in the upper South. The height of this mortarless construction is limited by how high the rock can be stacked without toppling; the natural limit on height provides a natural scale.

3–3. Cravens Hall, The University of the South, Sewanee, Tennessee.

3–2. Private residence, Nashville.

Wood sizes are determined by the size and nature of trees, which are linear not only in shape but in grain and, therefore, in strength. Wood also has the quality of nailability, which affects not only the way pieces of wood can be joined to each other and to other materials, but also wood's qualities of texture and appearance.

Wood grain constitutes one of the most familiar patterns and textures that can be derived from either finished building materials or that source we call "nature." Even when we are not close enough to distinguish the particular grain, we can often recognize wood. It provides easily and universally understood scalar clues, and it communicates these to us distinctly and powerfully. The texture, grain, and natural size of the wood siding-and-pole construction shown in figure 3–5 (along with the steps and handrail) help establish scale. Scale of a different but equally powerful sort is seen in figure 3–6, in which wood's structural capabilities make a forceful statement.

3–5. Appalachian Center for Crafts, DeKalb County, Tennessee.

3–4. Fence along Granny White Pike, Nashville.

3–6. Sea wall, Virginia Beach, Virginia.

Concrete, a material with the capacity for great variety and flexibility of application, can be used with clarity, integrity and forcefulness to express scale. The material's natural structural vigor can be seen in figures 3–7 and 3–8, as can its potential for presenting graceful and sensitive forms. The sizes of concrete members or parts tell us about the building's overall structure and the loads it is carrying. The plasticity of the material—another natural quality—allows the sensitive and adept designer to use it in very positive scale-expressive ways.

Steel, too, has rich potential for offering scalar clues. The steel construction shown in figure 3–9 provides the same general type of scalar information as concrete would, but in a way that differs significantly in character and content because of the different natures of the materials.

Another frequently encountered material capable of communicating about scale is clay roof tile, which is shown in several later illustrations in this book (figures 5–20, 7–7, 7–17, and 8–2). Originally, these tiles were formed by laying a sheet of wet clay

3–7. Olin Hall, Vanderbilt University, Nashville.

3–8. Jordan-Hare Stadium, Auburn University, Auburn, Alabama.

3–9. Jordan-Hare Stadium, Auburn University, Auburn, Alabama.

over a man's thigh, automatically and anatomically creating the shape, and helping to link the building material's scale to the human body.

Buildings in which different materials are used in combination frequently communicate to us about scale more completely than those in which one material is dominant. This is because the scalar qualities of different materials interact and reinforce each other. Figures 3–1 and 3–2 illustrate this phenomenon quite clearly. The tendency of building materials trade associations to promote the use of their products to the exclusion of others—for example, through awards programs for buildings using one dominant exterior material, such as brick or precast concrete—may artificially push designers in the direction of uniformity.

Equally unfortunate is the promotion of these same design values by some architectural educators and by some segments of the architectural press. Many buildings that receive recognition as a result of these promotional efforts are in fact worthy, but the profession as a whole would be better served if the same buildings were evaluated on a broader, more inclusive basis nearer to architecture's true purposes—which do not include the promotion of specific building products. If architecture is to achieve completeness of scale, it must be free to use its entire inventory of tools and means.

Another means by which we can observe the scale-giving qualities of materials is by the work they do in place. A general relationship exists between the size of a structural member—column, beam, arch, truss—and the load it is carrying. This size relationship is obviously not the same for all materials; and designers reserve the right to adjust the dimensions

(almost always by enlarging them) to achieve a desired visual effect.

It is readily evident, even without serious formal study of structural principles, that a column on the interior of a building will carry twice the load carried by a similar column on the exterior, and that one on an exterior corner will carry only one-fourth the load carried by the interior column. Theoretically, at least, the size of the column should reflect this difference, but frequently all columns are made the same size because the designer anticipates the uneasiness that people would feel at seeing some columns smaller than others. Though this certainly may be a legitimate concern, structural members do for the most part maintain a general relationship to their loads.

What all this means to scale is that size-to-load relationships can be used by architects to reinforce the overall sense of "fitness" that a building projects. If we intuitively understand something about the magnitude of the weight or force in a structure by observing or being conscious of the size of the structural elements (a matter of scale), then we have gained some generally reliable information about the form, the space, and the mass of the building.

Part of the sense of scale we experience involves sensing the weight or mass above and around us. If we stand inside a multistory parking structure—a building typically characterized by low ceilings and very heavy, massive structural members—we can understand the nature of the space, and of the form and mass, even if we can see only a small part of it. Further, if we observe light, slender columns and beams in place of massive supports in this same location, we sense either that there is not a parking structure above where we stand or that something is wrong. In other words, the structure either communicates reliably about its nature or is "out of scale."

Aside from gaining direct, technical knowledge about the physics of structural design, architectural and engineering students taking courses on the subject can also come to appreciate the potential for a system of insights, of subconscious feeling, in the "fitness" of structural choices. These choices, after being conceived, can then be tested by the technical procedures learned on a more conscious level. In the process, students may also gain understanding (though perhaps not consciously) of scale as it relates to structural design.

Closely related to materials actually used in buildings themselves are elements we find in the natural world, such as plants and topographic forms. Most people respond in similar, positive ways to familar plants forms—trees, shrubs, and even grass lawns.

Plants and landscaping have long been appreciated for their ability to enhance the attractiveness of buildings. They do this in part by introducing into the constructed assemblage a natural, green, fresh contrast of elements presented in their natural state. This attractiveness is enhanced when familiar types and sizes of plantings are used. Figure 3–10 shows the scale-giving effects of introducing shrubs and other

3–10. Private residence, Nashville.

plant forms to a typical residence. They not only dress up the foundation of the building, but also work to *found* the building's scale.

Most of us recognize the natural range of sizes exhibited by the leaves of common trees such as oak, maple, hickory, and pine—although every region will have its own list. Some of us can even recognize the natural range of sizes and shapes of other tree parts (as well as whole trees): the profile in winter or summer, the bark, and the configuration of the limbs. Each of these can give us clues to scale. The same is true in greater or lesser degree of smaller plants. Trees of various kinds set the scale for their locales and may even give visible form to invisible elements, as the trees

on the California coast near Monterey (figure 3–11) do the wind.

Topographic features of the earth, both in general form and in specific character (grassy meadow, rocky cliff, beach, and so on) inform us about scale. There is a natural range of sizes in the elements that compose many topographic forms, and experience has educated most of us about them. Thus, we understand their size and better comprehend the scale of other elements and objects found in their company. An example can be seen in figure 3–12, where a beach, including indigenous vegetation, rock formations, and of course the waves, cannot avoid expressing its scale.

3–11. Coastline, near Monterey, California.

3–12. Beach, Monterey, California.

Everyone who has studied architectural history has observed in the architecture of ancient and classical civilizations the transformation of forms from nature—particularly from the plant world—into stylized and systematized building features. Some of the impetus for this development came in the changeover from the use of plant materials still more or less in their natural state to the use of other, more durable materials that still retained a similarity of form to natural entities. However, another (possibly subconscious) motivation for this development may well have been a desire to maintain the scale-giving character provided by familiar plant forms—representatives of the known forms from nature that speak to all people.

Human beings share a perception of the surrounding world that constantly relates and compares external forms to the more or less measurable dimensions of the human body. Le Corbusier and others have fashioned systems of measurement and proportion based on the human body. The body is the one physical entity that unites and unifies us with all other human beings; and this particular kind of unity can be seen as a strong, essential, fundamental source of understanding about scale.

Most of our knowledge of the physical world comes by means of visual observation as we pass through it. Except for a few rare experiences—such as riding in a glass-walled elevator, a ferris wheel, a hang-glider, or a parachute—the way we obtain this knowledge is from a vantage point with a very narrow vertical range of heights above ground level. For adults, this usual range is from about 4 feet above the floor when seated to about 5½ feet above the floor when standing or walking—a difference of only about 18 to 24 inches. Although we can and do look up or down occasionally or tilt our heads slightly to enlarge our horizontal view, our basic viewing orientation is almost gyroscopically aligned to the horizontal. We unconsciously search for the horizon, even as we search for the sun. It is a constant and very literal datum line for every seeing human being.

At least part of the reason for this orientation is gravity, which is also the basis of structural necessity and design. When transported to a gravity-free environment, such as in astral space, human beings may lose this innate orientation to the horizontal. However, I believe that, as Voltaire said of God, if we did not have a horizon, it would be necessary to invent one. In any case, until called upon to design habitats in outer space, we must continue to design for man's horizon-seeking nature in accordance with the very real constraints of gravity.

Our horizontal plane is not, of course, at a constant elevation above sea level: it moves with us, as we ascend or descend. This fact opens to us another set of options in designing for scale, including possibilities growing out of consideration of the notions of heirarchy or sequence (discussed in chapter 4), of rhythm/repetition, precedence/emphasis, and tension (discussed in chapter 5), and of time (discussed in chapter 6). As these topics are discussed in turn, we should think of them in light of this phenomenon, identifying the options for design suggested by the fact that our perceived horizontal plane always exists in a close parallel to the ground on which we are standing at that moment.

Ascending or descending almost always entails moving from our baseline (the flat plane of the earth) toward some *thing*, some climactic place. In an enclosed stairwell, most of us experience a feeling fairly close to disorientation if we do not keep moving, either up or down. It is hard to know where we are, especially if no windows are present and more than two or three floors are served by the stairway. Whatever the scientific explanation for this effect may be, intuition points to the notion that when we are not moving, we seek the assurances of security that a spacious, flat horizontal plane gives us, whereas when we are in motion, we focus on the definite goal toward which we are moving—whether it be the next step on a stair or (more usually) another place where a spacious flat horizontal plane can be found.

The other basis of scale founded on the human body arises from our awareness of our own physical size and of the relation of everything else to that size. This applies not only to the 5- to 6-foot height of the typical adult but also to the spread of our arms, the comfortable length of a stride or height of a step, the size of an object that can be firmly gripped in one hand. The examples of bricks and cement blocks given earlier show how this influence manifests itself. A door knob, both in its size and in its height, provides another example. Using standards derived from the dimensions of our physical bodies, we establish our territory and carry it with us.

The height and breadth of a stairstep are essentially linked to human size, both to the size of a foot and to the length of a footstep. As a result, stairsteps communicate scale, as can be seen in figure 3–13. In this figure, we can also see the effect of using brick to reinforce our understanding of the scale of the steps and of the building they serve.

In Figure 3–14, the height and sensitive detailing of the handrail make it humanly accessible and visu-

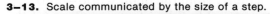

3–13. Scale communicated by the size of a step.

ally attractive, even though it is located in a monumental setting. On the other hand, a monumental interior stair (figure 3–15) can result when the height of the rail is correct but the cross-sectional size is unusually large. The outsized rail is hard to grip and therefore tends to intimidate us, implying monumental scale.

Figure 3–16, in another interior view, shows a close-up of a church pulpit; the height of the bookrests on it relates directly to the human body. Even when there is no one behind the pulpit, we understand the scale of this object, and by extension we understand the scale of the room in which it stands.

Sensitivity to the subtleties of scale is crucial at the personal level—where the individual, the building, and the ground all come together, where a person can experience a tactile relationship to a building's surfaces without actually having to touch them. The size of a doorway, when designed in proper scale, tells us much about what lies within, as well as about the heirarchy of architectural values in and about the building. The impression it makes largely results from its way of relating to the human figure—its manner of addressing us as creatures of finite size. This message is augmented by other aspects or variables such as shape, detail, and treatment of surfaces and edges.

A doorknob (figure 3–17) has its own scale-giving qualities. It must be the correct size for the human hand to grasp, and it must be the correct height above the floor to allow easy and comfortable operation. Likewise, a doorway must be a minimum size for human beings to pass through.

Every building has at least one point at which human beings approach it and come into direct, in-

3–14. Belmont United Methodist Church, Nashville.

3–15. Main stair, Tennessee State Capitol, Nashville.

3–16. First Christian Church, Glasgow, Kentucky.

timate contact with it; usually this occurs at many points or even along the entire perimeter. At these places, forces of intimate scale come into play which must be recognized and dealt with if a successful building is to result. Notice that my focus here is not on producing a "successful design": if a building does not welcome human beings in terms (that is, in a scale) they find familiar and comfortable, it is not a successful building, regardless of the merits of its abstracted qualities of design.

Our perceptions differ at different distances, and scalar elements speak to us in different ways from these different distances. The closer we get to a building, the more important the very personal and intimate levels of human physical relationship become—for example, the relationship in size of a part of the building to a part of our anatomy. Conversely, the farther we are from the building, the less important these concerns become and the more important grow those relating to nonhuman factors. In successful and complete design for architectural scale, the different sources of scale must all be recognized, accommodated, and integrated into a whole that is balanced in concept and execution.

Finally, another very basic source of scale should be noted before we move on: expectation. Expectation is grounded on our past experience and pervades our perception of all the other sources discussed in this chapter. Our experience leads us to expect that a brick will be a certain definite width and within an inch or two of a certain definite length. Likewise, we expect wood siding to fall within a certain range of sizes because we have seen so much that does. Although technologically it may be possible and practical to

3–17. Scale communicated by a doorknob and by the size of a doorway.

manufacture outsized bricks or synthetic products that fulfill at a magnified level the same function as wood siding, we would be disturbed by these (at least for a while) because they deny our expectations. Sometimes designers, for reasons they deem valid, intentionally distort the natural sizes of building elements. This would be an example of us being manipulated through our expectations—which is neither good nor bad in itself.

Both as architects and as observers, we must learn to master our expectations rather than allowing them to master us. We can do this by recognizing their origin in our own finite, fallible, and continuously evolving experience. At the same time that experience inexorably reshapes our thinking, it also reenforces many of our original premises and often encourages us to fall back on reflex responses in assessing new (and old) phenomena. Acknowledging this, we can direct the reshaping of our ideas responsibly by making the effort to select consciously our reaction to new experiences, by asking ourselves objective questions, and by seeking objective answers—in other words, by honing through practice our critical judgment.

4. Functions and Qualities of Scale

Scale in architecture has many functions, but the primary one is to communicate to the user/observer specific vital facts and notions about the nature of the building that are not fully provided by other aspects of physical form (size and shape, for example).

Although (if scale is viewed simply as a systematic expression of measurement) size could be characterized as a function or part of scale, the resulting notions of size and scale would be incomplete and inadequate. Size and scale are interdependent, but each involves considerably more than the features of the other that it mirrors. This is particularly true of scale.

The most general function of scale is to communicate the nature of a building or a space by evidencing the designer's consideration and discretionary use of the architectural variables at hand: materials, technology, form, size, color, texture—in short, the elements and principles of design.

Interrelated with this primary function are the subordinate, specific, and fulfilling qualities. These include:

☐ Qualities informative of a building's context (those relating a building to its setting);

☐ Qualities informative of the relation of a building's parts to its whole and to each other;

□ Qualities informative of a building's openness or lack thereof;

□ Qualities informative of a building's monumentality or diminutiveness;

□ Qualities informative of the hierarchy of spaces or parts or of the sequence of movement within and about a building;

□ Qualities informative of the critical cultural associations and historical allusions to be found in a building; and

□ Qualities subliminally informative of character, including the very special type of character (summed up in the word "greatness") to be found in landmark buildings such as the Taj Mahal, Fallingwater, Notre Dame, and Hagia Sophia.

CONTEXT

The meaning of context as used here is the setting into the midst of which a building is placed: the building's site, its natural and built environment, and its building or nonbuilding neighbors.

A great deal of architectural activity has been discussed under the heading of "contextualism." Although the term has been invoked at one level as an excuse for relying entirely on the tried-and-true formulas represented by the classical orders and other architectural traditions, at another level it describes a springboard for serious design decisions and imaginative, contemporary choices.

The recent addition to a preexisting church, both shown in figure 4–1, pays homage to the older building through its use of the same building materials, and through the form selected for the windows—which the viewer is not surprised to encounter in this context. A different expression is offered in figure 4–2, in which a new small office building (on the right) successfully mimics the massing of its two older house neighbors, and so manages to complement their scale.

4–1. Woodmont Baptist Church, Nashville.

4-2. Right: Patten Construction Company office building; others: private residences; Nashville.

The function of scale in terms of context is to aid the designer in establishing an appropriate relationship between new and old at locations that share a visual field. Obviously, if two buildings are not simultaneously visible, then their contextual relationship to each other is quite limited, if it exists at all—the only valid contextual relationship being one in which each building constitutes an event in a single processional sequence of buildings.

Contextualism will therefore be discussed from this point forward exclusively with regard to settings in which an observer can stand in one spot—or at the very most, move casually around at will—and see and understand a building in its immediate environment.

A designer trying to resolve the contextual issues of scale should start by determining the scale or scales of the environment in which the new construction is to occur, as well as the other preexisting features to which the new building must relate. Then the designer must decide *how* the new building should relate to its neighbors and setting.

Should it dominate or be subordinate? Should it

be played off against the existing structures by contrasting with them in color, form, and materials, or should it fit in by using the same colors, forms, and materials? Should it mirror the forms and expressions of its older neighbors, or reinterpret them, or studiously ignore them? Should it accommodate existing circulation patterns, or should it seek to modify or totally change them? Will the imposition of new construction change the ways the existing buildings relate to their setting? If so, should the design of the new building attempt to compensate for the change, or are there larger, overriding concerns that justify subordinating this question? What characteristics should be given to the exterior spaces the new building will create?

PARTS

The parts of a building include major masses, openings, voids, bases or caps of a single mass or volume, and areas of different color, texture, or material. Considered from a single vantage point, these parts might correspond to those involved in a painter's concept of composition; certainly they affect how the facade of a building "composes." In a similar way, considered three-dimensionally, the parts could correspond to those in a sculptor's notions of composition. In either case, they are very close to the ideas on composition taught in basic (abstract) design courses.

Other goals must be met by architectural scale besides these purely formal ones, however: making the building sensitive to its proposed uses; responding to concerns of energy conservation through passive and active strategies; meeting the owner's construction budget; and so on. Some of these goals are fulfilled by the other qualities identified in this chapter. Using the relationships presented by a building's parts to meet these goals in a way that appropriately considers scale is both an opportunity and a responsibility for the designer.

The parts visible in figure 4–3 seem harmonious because all are based on simple geometric figures, are rendered in a limited palate of materials—brick, wood, mullionless glass, and metal roofing—and fall into a relatively narrow range of sizes. By contrast, while the parts seen in figure 4–4 are based on only slightly more complex forms and use a similar range of materials, they express a compositional heirarchy because of the wide difference in size among the parts.

OPENNESS

One of the qualities of a building most readily felt by the viewer is the openness, confinedness, or closure

4–3. Hampton Place Condominiums, Nashville.

4–4. Woodmont Baptist Church, Nashville.

it conveys. The careful proportioning of voids to solids is one of the designer's most useful tools. Basic choices about voids and solids obviously affect feelings about a building's scale, but so do subtler choices about voids and solids, such as how transitions between void and solid will be treated and how variations in size and character of openings at different levels or places in a building will be arranged. The questions to be addressed in considering open versus solid relationships can be restated most basically as questions of welcoming (or forbidding) and of sheltering (or either leaving unprotected or turning away).

The contrast between openness and closure can be seen in figures 4–5 and 4–6. The sheltered all-glass entrance of the small, commercial building (figure 4–5) welcomes the viewer, inviting entry. Few if any secrets are withheld: everything is open to inspection from without, and as a result nothing untranslatable or unknown remains to threaten us. The deadly blankness of the other building wall (figure 4–6) not only turns people away but gives them few if any scalar clues.

Intentionally designing for a closed, protective aspect can certainly be appropriate and a legitimate design objective, however, in various situations. For example, strict limits on a building's degree of openness are in order when the purpose of the building does not include expressing a general welcome to the public passing by, or when the privacy of the occupants and the activities carried on in the building is a significant design consideration. This objective can be obtained without sacrificing scalar details when pursued by a sensitive architect.

4–5. Crestmoor Building, Nashville.

4–6. A closed public face on a building.

4—7. Olin Hall, Vanderbilt University, Nashville.

MONUMENTALITY OR DIMINUTIVENESS

Another basic way in which an entire building assemblage relates to human beings is indicated by the extremes of overwhelming them (through monumentality) or of making them feel disproportionately large (through diminutiveness). By monumentality, I mean a building's quality or character of tending to make the viewer/user feel smaller and less significant in relation to the structure than would seem justified by the mere physical relationship of overall sizes. Diminutiveness refers to the opposite quality or character—one tending to make us feel larger and more significant in relation to the structure. Legitimate reasons exist for pursuing either extreme; indeed, most buildings that satisfy us visually and emotionally include qualities of both monumentality and diminutiveness, which are balanced through a broad range of scalar attributes.

By their very nature, monumentality and diminutiveness affect the human viewer in an extraordinarily personal way. It is therefore extremely important that the statement these qualities make is handled sensitively and skillfully by the designer. The size of the building shown in figure 4–7 can clearly be seen by the rows of windows, each expressing a floor. However, the size and aspect of the individual elements—the sweeping columns, the sloping spandrels, and the blank ends—combine to overwhelm us and to lessen the building's human sympathy. The nineteenth century city house (figure 4–8) expresses the opposite quality, diminutiveness, by the smallness of its elements, by its intimate details and surface treatments, and by its modest and appropriate overall size. Another variety of diminutiveness can be seen in figure 4–9, in which similar treatments of detail to those seen in figure 4–8, along with design measures taken to break the mass down visually into smaller parts, result in a relatively large building appearing intimate in aspect.

4–8. Nineteenth-century city house, Nashville.

4–9. Old Gymnasium, now Department of Art, Vanderbilt University, Nashville.

HIERARCHY OR SEQUENCE

"Hierarchy" signifies not only a range of sizes or other physical characteristics but also a range of importance and (by extension) an order implied and imposed in accordance with that range; this resulting order is "sequence." In many building designs, one objective is to direct people from the point of entry along a prescribed pathway to a desired terminus. Directing may be attempted by uses of scale wholly on the outside of the building or wholly on the inside; in the best examples, it is usually attempted both inside and out.

The ordering device may be as mundane as a system of corridors in an office building or as dramatic as a series of spatial variations in a High Gothic church. Scale can help establish and reinforce the sequence, the spatial compressions and releases, and other devices used in developing sequence and movement—as well as helping to shape the individual events in the sequence so that the objectives of the entire processional are properly served.

Figures 4–10 and 4–11 illustrate static, symmetrical expressions of hierarchy and sequence in which the elements of the buildings are organized to focus attention on the entrances, with lesser importance being accorded to other elements, forms, and surfaces in a sort of radial pattern over the facade.

Figures 4–12 and 4–13 illustrate more dynamic expressions of hierarchy and sequence. Being strongly linear, they propel us along. In figure 4–12, even though our viewpoint is at the climax of the progression, the path of movement and the major modes along the way are clear to us. In figure 4–13, the sequence itself may be more important than the climax.

4–10. Falls School, Nashville.

4–11. Hume-Fogg High School, Nashville.

4-12. Legislative Plaza, Nashville.

4-13. Arcade, Tripoli, Libya.

CULTURAL ASSOCIATION

Modern architecture originally frowned on using formal associations from past experiences in designs—for example, echoing the lines of a barn in the whole form of a church building. Similarly, forms derived from nature were generally discouraged. Both types of architectural allusion offended orthodox Modern theory because they represented visual or formal links with the past or with other sources external to the purpose, function, and use of the building.

One of the benefits of the recent questioning of the tenets of Modernism has been to remove the stigma that once automatically attached to designs that gave expression to cultural associations.

Without knowing more than can be deduced from looking at the picture of the building shown in figure 4–14, there are several facts about the building we can state with reasonable certitude: it is a church building, probably (because of its traditional and rather ornate style) for one of the more liturgical denominations, and it likely was built before World War II. These are typical bits of information that cultural associations can tell us.

Much of what has been done under the new freedom to make cultural associations, unfortunately, has consisted of a rather random plucking of disparate ornaments from history, which are then stuck on buildings as though they were birthday cake decorations. Historical reference is certainly justifiable, but it ought not be enlisted for capricious reasons or whimsical effects (unless whimsey itself serves a legitimate purpose in the particular design effort). The use of cultural associations in building design also should not serve merely to mirror the forms, details, or materials of existing buildings nearby, or to play off these buildings for no effect other than a kind of gentle visual satire. Their best use goes deeper and attempts to discover and reinterpret to society important and contextually relevant cultural values and ideas the designer recognizes in the scale and features of the historical models.

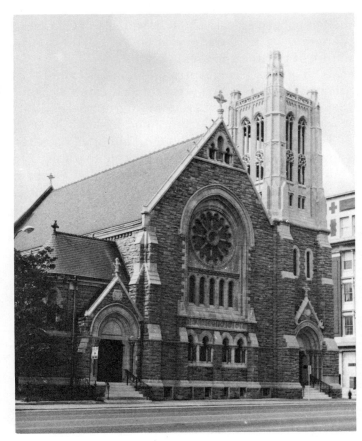

4–14. Christ Episcopal Church, Nashville.

GREATNESS

Greatness is not a quality of the same breadth and kind as parts, context, and the other qualities of scale discussed thus far; rather, it is a rare and remarkable species of a quality we might call "character." Unfortunately, character—perhaps because it comprehends so vast a range of potential expressions—does not readily admit fruitful inquiry. Without engaging in ineffectual generalities about the quality of character, therefore, let us focus our attention on the special nature of greatness in architecture.

The most frequently recognized aspect of greatness of the Taj Mahal is primarily external, while that of the Hagia Sophia is primarily internal; Fallingwater and Notre Dame are noted for both internal and external greatness, although Fallingwater is best known from a very famous exterior photograph. This enumeration only serves to underscore that elements of greatness can infuse both the external and the internal aspects of a building.

A very common feature of buildings that are recognized as great is a *major* space. Churches, railroad and airport terminals, theaters, and other assembly spaces achieve greatness in numbers disproportionate to their representation in the entire inventory of buildings at least in part because of their successful treatment of major spaces.

While they cannot adequately convey the majesty of the building itself, figures 4–15 and 4–16 may give a small hint of the overwhelming grandeur of this sixth century Byzantine masterpiece (the minarets were added in the fifteenth century). On the exterior, the parts mass themselves not only in astounding visual magnificence, but also in near-perfect structural logic and order. The clutter of more recent, lower structures nestling around the outside of the building makes the exterior more difficult to comprehend than the interior.

The interior offers one of the world's greatest spatial experiences—the paragon of major spaces. Bannister Fletcher writes, "Scale is obtained by the gradation of the various parts, from the two-storied arcades of the aisles to the lofty dome which rests, with little apparent support, like a canopy over the centre."*

The character and success of a major space, as well as of subordinate or "servant" spaces, is largely determined by the skill used in the application of scale-giving techniques of design; these techniques also serve as principal determinants of the character and success of other building features. Whether a building has achieved greatness or not can probably be accurately gauged only after many years. Many buildings celebrated in the recent past have not sustained their reputations over time and now seem only quaint, or even ugly.

In most design situations, a conscious striving for greatness is (perhaps paradoxically) unwise. A more appropriate aim is to design the *best* building that can be produced out of the opportunity the commission represents. Nevertheless, the qualities of character discoverable in buildings that society has recognized as great can speak to us and (to some extent) direct us. Many of these qualities, we will probably find, express scalar ideas.

*A History of Architecture on the Comparative Method, 17th ed. New York: Charles Scribner's Sons, 1963.

4-15. Hagia Sophia, Istanbul, Turkey.

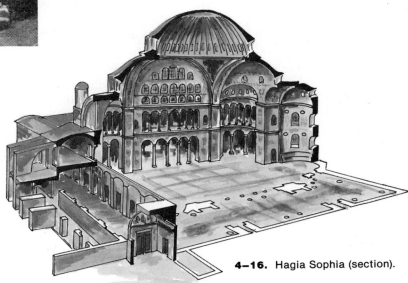

4-16. Hagia Sophia (section).

Perhaps this chapter which addresses the functions of scale is an appropriate place to address the Modern credo, "Form follows function." The edict is simple and weighty, and to several generations of architects, it embodied perhaps the highest truth. After two decades of practical survival and observation of what really gets built, however, I find that this maxim makes sense only if the definition of function is stretched to include much more than the generally understood content of "function." The definition must include, for example, the visually functional as well as the operationally functional. And if it is to identify buildings that are functional through the broadest range of usefulness to their human occupants, the definition must entertain such questions as: does the building invite habitation? are the floor area and arrangement satisfactory for performing the narrowly defined work planned for the building?

The idea of the visually functional opens up an entirely new area of investigation, analysis, and choice for the designer. Its sphere is qualitative, whereas that of the standard Modern definition of function is quantitative. In order to gauge the visually functional, the designer must discover and understand a new set of values and make judgments about them. Part of a building's visual function might be to unite disparate existing elements in the environment, or to prepare the user/observer—by means of a progression through spaces—for some climactic experience, or to make the user/observer feel calm, comforted, excited, enthusiastic, at ease, introspective, or patriotic.

Another major aspect of this expanded definition is technical function: not the measurement of space, but the work the building actually does for itself, such as holding itself up (structure) or heating and cooling itself (environmental control).

Could this be what Louis Sullivan actually intended when he spoke of form following function: that the doctrine can serve as a universal parameter for determining all of the requirements applicable to a particular building, and for putting the requirements into proper balance one with another? Certainly Sullivan had much to say about ornament and its service to the purposes of the whole. The broad definition of function identified here requires more preparatory effort on the part of the designer, but perhaps it will result in better work.

While older philosophies of design often undertake to justify design choices on the basis of either ratiocination or formal intuition (rarely does a conscientious architect venture very far from either of these extremes), the designer using scale to its fullest potential—which means taking advantage of all of its functional possibilities—has the option of responding to and utilizing any point of view along the entire continuum between them. The scale-conscious designer can let intuition freely guide the direction of planning, while simultaneously refining the plan particulars by means of rational application of the tools of scalar design, in total service to explicitly stated design goals. This, I believe, provides a way of directing architecture back to its basics, without losing the force or even the essential direction of modern advances and developments.

5. Elements and Principles of Scale

Traditionally in the abstract study of design, a distinction is made between principles and elements of design. Elements comprise aspects of the physical reality of the structure or other object being designed: line, form, color, texture, patterns, light, and so forth in the general case; and such things as doors, windows, and walls in the particular case of building forms. Principles, on the other hand, describe the relationships possible through manipulating or expressing those elements: rhythm, repetition, symmetry, balance, proportion, dominance, subordination, tension, variety, and unity, among others.

Rather than overemphasize the distinctions between these two concepts, we will concentrate on the special characteristics of each element or principle identified, without particular regard for whether it might best be labeled one or the other. In discovering how scale works in architectural design, the designer must learn to evaluate every applicable variable with equal objectivity. Rhythm, for example, should be given equally weighted consideration—in terms of its potential use as a scale-giving principle—with color or texture.

The elements and principles of scale identified in this chapter are not arranged hierarchically; however, an order of preference devised for a specific building design may very well be desirable or even necessary.

Applying elements and principles to a specific design or building is a matter of extreme complexity. Of equal complexity are the interactions among various elements and principles. Decisions about one of these variables affect all, and the effectiveness of one in producing the desired sense of scale may either enhance or diminish the effectiveness of another.

Some of the elements and principles discussed below are treated in pairs. Playing opposing or complementary concepts off one another often helps clarify both, and this is what is being attempted here.

LINE/EDGE

In architecture, a line frequently can be generated by the edge of one or more forms. Sometimes, line is created by a change of color or material in the same plane or by the addition of a device (such as an iron railing or neon tubing) applied to the basic form of a building. Line may also be found in the visual boundary of a form seen against its background—as in the case of an unexpected but appropriate roofline. Figure 5–1 shows an example of such a memorable line generated by an integrated roof form. The domed roof of this building retains the same line when seen against the sky from any point on the compass, forcefully impressing its distinct character on the mind of the viewer.

A similar expression can be seen in figure 5–2, in which the manipulation of the applied facade produces a similarly striking effect, but only when viewed from one direction.

Edges, like lines, constitute an extremely useful group of variables for the designer. A meeting of two dissimilar materials or an abrupt change in direction by a plane or other simple form produces an edge.

5–1. Green Hills office, Commerce Union Bank, Nashville.

5–2. Tempo's Restaurant, Nashville.

Edges provide a multitude of visual and scalar clues about our distance from and size relationships to the surfaces, which then help us to establish formal priorities for visually organizing the elements in the whole building harmoniously.

An edge associated with a single material relies for its definition and effects on the play of light and shadow. An edge that occurs at the meeting of different materials relies more heavily on differences in color, texture, size of each unit, and other elements of the materials for its resolution. If both a change of direction and a change of material occur along the same edge, an even richer division of form is possible.

We should cultivate the habit of looking thoughtfully at the edges we see in buildings around us. What is happening at a given edge and why? What happens when the distance from which it is viewed changes? What effects would be produced if the materials were changed? Would the change improve or worsen the edge's contribution to the overall scale of the building?

The nature of an edge is closely related to the nature of the material that forms it. Cut stone, for example, being (usually) large and rectilinear, has an edge that is distinctly different from edges formed by wood, brick, metal, and glass.

Examples of edges can be seen in figures 5–3 through 5–5. Figure 5–3 shows the edge formed by two dissimilar materials in the same plane; figure 5–4 shows edges created by a minor but distinct shift in planes composed of the same material (brick), reinforced by a change in pattern; figure 5–5 shows two types of edges—one that is formed by a change of color in the same plane and material, and one by an abrupt change in direction.

5–3. Private residence, Nashville.

5–4. Green Hills Post Office, Nashville.

5–5. Target Store, Nashville.

5–6. First Christian Church,
Glasgow, Kentucky.

FORM/MASS

Closely related to line and edge is the notion of form. The most basic use of the word "form" (sometimes called "shape" instead) is to mean the massing of the building in its major parts. It can also refer to the particular shaping of the various smaller parts that contribute to the whole.

The architect's treatment of the smaller parts is at least as decisive in producing a desirable scale in the building as is the treatment of the major masses because the human body relates more easily to a smaller object than to an entire building. Indeed, the most valuable role of the smaller parts may be to serve as a linking mechanism between the viewer (a human being) and the whole. The building shown in figure 5–6 illustrates this well: not only does the basic form of the building express acoustical and spatial needs directly and lyrically, but also the various smaller parts—such as steps, handrails, doors, and windows—serve to link all into a comprehensible whole and to relate this whole to human size. The way the form relates to its context can also serve to establish scale for the viewer. See also figure 4–2.

To most of us, mass means something that is slightly different from form—sort of the basic lump or bulk of a building in its most elementary state, its most easily perceived whole or total state. This means that, in the case of many (and perhaps most) buildings, the mass or massing can only be perceived at some distance, as is the case in figure 5–7. Unfortunately, many buildings (in urban settings particularly) cannot be easily seen in totality at middle distances simply because they are located in crowded environments. In such cases, the close-up forms are likely to be the most important (and indeed, the only) ones that have a scalar impact.

Scale is difficult for even the most experienced and perceptive of us to discern from city skyline distances. Forms and masses can be seen, understood, and enjoyed from such distances, but they will convey very little sense of actual scale.

5–7. Gould-Turner Group offices, Nashville.

SPACE

Particularly in its proportioning and size, space produces scalar effects. As used here and elsewhere in this book, space denotes the palpable volume contained by tangible or implied constructions. An example of implied construction is the open side of a stage; the space on and within the stage would not be perceived to extend beyond the stage's front, even though there is nothing physical there to "stop" it.

Other variables can and should be used to modify and enhance the scalar qualities of space, but space provides the basic field within which these other variables are positioned. We have all experienced the feeling of disorientation and uneasiness produced by entering a large space in which the ceiling was low relative to the horizontal dimensions, or in which some of the horizontal limits of space seemed not to be present because of a general looseness in spatial form or an absence of prominent space-defining elements. These are instances in which space has been poorly handled or intentionally enlisted to achieve an unsettling effect.

Space exists inside and outside buildings, around and between buildings. It is the element to which human beings most fundamentally react when experiencing their environment: they do not react to walls, floors, or ceilings, but rather to the spaces these enclose, define, and shape.

One recurring idea in architectural thought is the belief that mankind emotionally needs to experience at intervals a "major space"—exterior as well as interior. If we provide no opportunity for people to do this (the argument continues), we may deprive them of some-thing essential to their mental health and may be guilty of adding to social problems with our building activity rather than helping to solve them. A properly and appropriately scaled "major space" may well be required by program in many building projects, but more importantly, *all* spaces—inside and out, major and subordinate, and the entirety of the building as well—should be scaled carefully and appropriately. Figures 5–8 and 5–9 show two examples, one large and one small, of gracefully handled major spaces.

Acoustic space, though seeming to apply primarily to interior spaces, can apply equally well to the exterior. It involves the quality of resonances we receive from surfaces—from sounds we generate as well as from those attributable to other people and to mechanical or other external sources. Two examples of exterior spaces of recognizable acoustical character

5–8. First Baptist Church, Nashville.

5–9. First Christian Church, Glasgow, Kentucky.

5–10. Church Street, Nashville.

are shown in figures 5–10 and 5–11. Figure 5–10 presents a typical urban street scene, readily calling to mind all of the noise generated by traffic and reverberated from the tall buildings; figure 5–11 presents an isolated courtyard in which the anticipated splash of the water from the fountain makes a major contribution to our acoustic and, therefore, total perception of the space.

We all know the sensations of space that can be gathered from the echoing of footsteps in cavernous, hard-clad spaces. Even if blindfolded, we can tell much about the extent and layout of a space just by the sound of our own footsteps. Other spaces (again, exterior as well as interior) have different acoustic qualities, which nonetheless operate on us in a similar way. In the room in figure 5–12, the padding of the rugs and overstuffed furniture temper the reverberant quality of the high enclosure and the hard surfaces of the glass wall, producing a unique but controlled acoustic environment.

Steen Eilen Rasmussen, in his book *Experiencing Architecture,** devotes a full chapter to "Hearing Architecture," in which he provides an excellent exposition of the acoustic qualities of space.

A knowledge of and sensitivity to the science of acoustics is necessary to the competent practice of architecture today. Often it is desirable to consult an acoustics specialist about a design, especially for such spaces as theaters and music halls where this component of the design process is vital. We must keep in mind that every space has *some* acoustic quality, and we must try to match that quality with the visual and other qualities we give the space in design.

* Boston: MIT Press, 1959.

5—11. Market, Guatemala City.

5—12. Private residence,
Franklin, Tennessee.

LIGHT/DARK

Light as a scale-shaping element is a double-edged sword because, at least on the exteriors of buildings, it is highly variable and beyond the control of the designer. When the sun is shining, it can be an extremely powerful animator to the forms and scalar properties of a building—one that the sensitive and confident designer will recognize, respect, and utilize. However, the effect of overcast and even rainy days on form and scale must be acknowledged and integrated into the design of buildings.

In some geographic and climatic regions, overcast skies may be more prevalent than clear ones; this, too, needs to be recognized and handled in a positive way. Many of the qualities of successful building forms in such regions resulted from designers' working with the quality and quantity of available natural light to enhance design goals instead of trying to deny or defy them.

One prominent example of this type of adjustment is the architectural vocabulary of French and English Gothic, which originated and blossomed in regions of frequent rain and overcast skies. The busyness, the agitated spikiness of the Gothic forms contribute immensely to their visual definition in the soft, hazy atmosphere of the countries in which they emerged. The great expanses of glass used in Gothic churches were attempts to gulp what little light there was into the building interiors; and the shape of the masonry superstructure surrounding and infilling the glass was planned in part to sharpen the form on the exterior. When such forms were transferred to sunnier climes, such as Spain's or Italy's, the results were

sometimes disastrous, producing buildings that seem to crawl and quiver in the intense, hot light and almost to come alive like giant spiders from a cheap monster movie.

Light in the interior of a building is more controllable by the designer, through artificial lighting or the control of natural light or both. Dramatic effect, as well as spatial order and scalar definition, can be produced and enhanced by the discriminating use and control of light. To leave lighting design totally in the hands of a lighting engineer is to relinquish a vital responsibility and to risk having choices made in lighting design that cancel out scalar effects obtained by other means and through other variables. The typical flooding of a space with bland, uniform, shadowless fluorescent light may be a viable choice for some or even many interior environments, but certainly not for all, and it will definitely wash out and negate the impact of many other design choices.

Dark may be defined simplistically as the absence of light, but it is really considerably more. Dark, as well as light, can be used elementally to achieve desired scalar effects. Light can be played against dark in an infinite variety of combinations; it is a basic way of providing an advancing/receding relationship between parts, a relationship of dominance/subordination, and a relationship involving tension, precedence, or emphasis. Figure 3–8, besides offering an example of the strength and versatility of concrete, shows a present-day expression of the interplay of light and shadow created by vigorous structural forms. In figure 5–13, we can see a more conventional display of light (reflected from the structure) in contrast with dark (the void of the window openings).

5–13. Nineteenth-century commercial buildings, Nashville.

Shadow as a shifting form of darkness has been understood and used since the earliest days of architecture to define form (particularly in sunlight), to establish essential links between structures and their human viewers, and to allow human beings to participate in the dynamics of scale in architecture.

Light from whatever source is the means by which we perceive architecture. Yet no matter how effectively and sensitively artificial lighting is used, it can never take the place of natural light from the sun. We lose first a sense of time when this connection is severed; and second, a sense of place. Sunlight is a dynamic force that acts on buildings and other forms with some level of strength and some recognizable character every day, whether we acknowledge it or not. Considered as a design principle, sunlight does

not simply drape itself passively over forms; it is called upon to participate actively in the design process.

Architecture students are commonly urged to take their models out into the sunlight to observe and try to comprehend what sunlight does to them and (if the teacher is wise) to see how designs can be refined to take maximum advantage of sunlight. And yet how often do we see this step taken in the design of actual buildings? Possibly because considerations of economics militate against such a practice, huge numbers of buildings have been designed and built with no regard whatsoever to what happens to them in sunlight.

We do not really need to build new models and carry them out into the sun to learn, though; all we have to do to begin the process of rediscovering sunlight is to go outdoors and look at some buildings—any buildings! Practically any building, when looked at with a critical eye, will tell us something worth knowing. It does not have to be a traditional building, although the traditional may be more likely to have the kind of detail that sunlight animates. Beginning the process means only taking the first step; what follows in the process should be an expression of our growth in critical judgment, as well as our knowledge about and facility in dealing with scale. I do not mean to encourage wholesale copying of traditional architectural forms ("instant archaelogy," I have heard it called), but lessons can be learned from them—especially from the classical orders and related forms.

In the United States, the closest thing we have to authentic Greek or Roman buildings are reproductions, such as the Nashville Parthenon (see figure 5–18). Nonetheless, thousands of buildings have been designed and built in our country that more or less resemble ancient models. This is attributable to the development of a codified language of forms and of rules for their use which could be applied with little or no original thought. Although these families of forms produced predictable results, they were frequently useful and satisfying, in part because their originators—the Greeks and Romans—had understood the effects of sunlight and had developed the original forms to respond to sunlight and maximize its benefits.

When we look at a reproduction of a classical building, we notice how sunlight clings to and heightens the contours of the moldings, especially in the bold examples that most closely approach the scale of the originals. Then too, we notice how this visual effect enhances scalar definition, providing a vital link to us, physically *and* emotionally, by identifying the sizes of the object and its parts. Figures 5–14 through 5–16 show three examples of the way sunlight plays over traditional moldings to add definition and scale.

The shafts of classical columns were often fluted (fluted and smooth forms are shown in figures 5–17 and 5–18). The practice of fluting columns may have developed as a means of concealing minor defects inherent in hand-crafted manufacture—defects whose visibility would have been greatest on the smooth,

5–14. Guatemala National Cathedral, Guatemala City.

5–16. Farmers Bank and Trust, Winchester, Tennessee.

ostensibly round shafts of unfluted columns. However, I believe a more important reason for preferring fluted columns was that they handled sunlight in an active and enlivening way, giving the viewer understandable subforms and a dimension within which to grip the larger forms visually.

When we contrast the columns on the buildings shown in figures 5–17 and 5–18, we see that even in strong sunlight the smooth cylindrical form exhibited in the first example lacks strong definition. However, the other example demonstrates not only sharper definition but also an unmistakable visual invitation to touch and attempt to grip the flutes. The flutes, therefore, constitute another scale-giving feature: one that among its other attributes tends to flesh out smaller regions in the range of scale discussed in chapter 6.

5–15. Masonic Grand Lodge Building, Nashville.

5–17. Belmont Heights Baptist Church, Nashville.

5–18. The Parthenon, Nashville.

COLOR

Color in building design, particularly on the exterior, is often a limited palate governed by the materials used. Using the "natural" range of colors available in building materials such as brick, stone, and some metals is one way to apply discipline to building design. "Natural" here means that no effort is made in the manufacturing process to alter the color produced by the constituent material or materials being used.

More and more construction materials are becoming available, however, that have no "natural" color. The manufacturer then has to make some decision about color at extra cost. In addition, some products are manufactured to look as much as possible like other, more natural materials; and the colors in which these products are offered for sale may resemble those found in the natural materials.

In any case, the designer needs to look carefully at the scale-giving potential of color choices. Just as with arrangements of light and dark, colors can make a surface advance or recede and can reinforce relationships of dominance and subordination. Many fine books on this extremely broad and complex topic are available and should be consulted for a thorough treatment of color issues.

The four color illustrations (figures C–1 through C–4 in the color section) offer examples of various scalar effects due to color. In the first, second, and fourth pictures, color provides sharper definition of form, helping us as viewers to define our physical relationship to the form. Sometimes, as in figures C–1 and C–2, the particular way of using color comes from a cultural tradition (one Hispanic and one Chinese, here). This need not, however, detract from the scale-giving potential the color has.

Figure C–3 shows a famous reproduction of a Roman villa. The use of color in this rather faithful copy may surprise those whose only contact with Greco-Roman antiquity comes from centuries-old sun- and wind-bleached stones or from black and white photographs. Nevertheless, color, and particularly applied color, did play an important part in this architecture, and one notable use of it was to embellish surfaces that were to be seen bathed in strong sunlight, so that their subtleties of form and definition could be more readily seen.

The National Theater in Guatemala City, shown in figure C–4, is itself a remarkable example of architectural "theater": it is sited atop a prominent hill, and its forms reflect the nearby range of volcanic mountains. The bold use of color here may have been an attempt by the designer to disguise or manipulate the theater's scale, to make the mass of the building seem to float above the hilltop and recede into the distance, intensifying the already dramatic effect the building has.

TEXTURE

Because of its multiplicity of form and its great potential for direct human response, texture is one of the most important elements a designer can use in establishing scale in buildings. If the texture of a surface is fine enough, a person is likely to sense it in a very intimate way, recognizing the physical relation of the textural unit to the human body and hand, and possibly also to human armspan and height.

This kind of readily discernible relationship is particularly important at the critical edge where the building meets the ground. Buildings, even monumental ones, should at ground level address the viewer in a most personal and direct way; and not with the bombastic oratory of self-conscious profundity, but in conversational tones—inviting, welcoming, making the person feel at ease and at home. Monumentality and expressions of grandeur and power can be stated and perceived from a distance. At close range, polite, unassuming gentility is needed to provide the humanizing and harmonizing balance that a work of good and complete architecture requires.

At ground level, a building should be almost huggable: it should present us with a surface or surfaces that we feel we could, if so inspired, physically embrace. Moreover, in many design situations, the building *should* inspire us to try to embrace it, by presenting a texture or range of textures that have the quality of inviting exploration of its surfaces.

Texture can be understood in both visual and tactile terms. Even though architecture as a form of expression may seem to be primarily a visual medium, other senses can be enlisted to complement sight in enriching our perception of scale. (The earlier discussion of acoustic space provides an example of this.) We know from past experience what the tactile quality of a familiar material is likely to be. The smoothness or roughness of a surface communicates to us, as does our own expectation of how the surface should feel—even when it is beyond our physical reach, and we must rely for sensation solely upon sight.

Another quality we experience through touch is the temperature of a surface, especially its temperature in comparison to the ambient air temperature. If we touch a smooth, hard surface in the presence of high ambient temperature, for example, we can (and most likely do, subconsciously) make a judgment about the nature and scale of the material. If this surface is relatively cool we assume the material is dense and thick, probably stone or concrete. This is because the mass of these materials slows their absorption of heat from the outside. If, on the other hand, this surface is hot, we assume the material is metal of a relatively thin dimension, because our past experience tells us that this material quickly and intensely absorbs ambient heat.

The texture of various materials and the effects they produce can be seen in figures 5–19 through 5–21, which show respectively brick, stone and clay tile, and ribbed concrete block constructions. Each has its own special qualities that communicate to us about the scale of the object on which they are found. This occurs in part because of our past associations with the materials and their "natural" textures, in part because of the visual relationship of the materials to other elements in the construction, and in part because of the texture itself.

Texture, I believe, is the most intimate form of language a building uses in communicating with us. It is the language of whispers and small talk, as well as the language of challenging conversation on serious subjects between friends. Texture provides surfaces we can literally "come to grips with" and seriously engage on an intellectual level. It is the means by which we establish the particular link with a building

C-1: Hotel courtyard, Antigua, Guatemala.

C–2: Office building,
Chinatown, San Francisco.

C–3: John Paul Getty Museum, Malibu, California.

C–4: National Theater, Guatemala City.

5–19. Hillsboro Church of Christ, Nashville.

5–20. Gateway, Sterling Court Apartments, Nashville.

American relief (figure 5–23), in the same tradition but using modern technology.

Since speech in any form and with any vocabulary constitutes communication, upholding the quality and coherence of communication that texture makes possible is essential in perceiving, understanding, and (on the designer's part) creating scale. The playful, participatory texture imparted to a park dragon skin, shown in figure 5–24, is an example of this kind of communication. The tile surface was installed by hundreds of people; anyone who came by and wished to participate was welcomed. This resulted in superb scale; it is instantly evident to us upon seeing the dragon that even if we did not personally lay any of the tile, we could have done so with perfectly harmonious results.

5–22. Quetzalcoatl Temple, Teotihuacan, Mexico.

(or even a part of a building) that at close range completes our scalar relationships with it. Without textural variety, our dialogue would be like a conversation with a robot that could only say one word or one short phrase. Textural variety, applied with a sensitive designer's skill, allows for an immense range of conversation.

The pre-Columbian carving shown in figure 5–22 is an example of articulating a surface (this applies to reliefs as well as to three-dimensional sculptures) in order to relate scale and to present important religious symbols. Compare this with the modern Central

5-23. Government Complex, Guatemala City.

5-24. Tile Dragon, Fanny Mae Dees Park, Nashville.

PATTERN

Pattern is established by the ordering of other principles and elements, from total form to texture to color. It consists of the arrangement of design elements in such a way that an identifiable arranged unit may be extended by repetition in two or more dimensions. Examples are the pattern in which a brick wall or walk is laid, the pattern of window muntins, or the pattern of joints betweeeen precast concrete panels on a building's face.

The physical size of the components required to produce an effective pattern depends on the distance from which the building is viewed. For example, the pattern of brick and mortar in a wall, except by association with color and other clues from our past experience, cannot be distinguished beyond a certain distance (about 200 feet, for most of us). The same can be said for standard patterns produced by most other common building materials, although the operative distances vary for specific materials. Therefore, if a visual pattern readable from greater distances is desired, an effort must be made to strengthen and enlarge the pattern or to make up a new pattern composed of larger building parts.

The ironwork patterns shown in figure 5–25,

5–25. Gazebo, Belmont College, Nashville.

working in concert with the viewers' likely knowledge
of the structural capabilities of the material, help
establish the scale of these twin gazebos; the distance
between them also can be readily perceived because
we understand the scale of each one.

Patterns in pavement enhance both movement
and visual or apparent distance; patterns on vertical
and overhead surfaces make them seem to advance or
retreat, or else contrast them with adjacent or nearby
surfaces, and perhaps also provide a way of introducing rhythm into the structure. In figure 5–26, we see a
variety of different materials and treatments in pav-
ing; brick, exposed aggregate concrete, granite setts,
and iron grating.

5–26. Capitol Boulevard,
Nashville.

5-27. Condominiums,
Guatemala City.

RHYTHM/REPETITION

Rhythm, borrowed from musical roots, is a time-based (and, therefore, linear) expression of balanced movement in a processional sense; it becomes perceptible as the viewer either physically moves by, through, or around a building or space, or visually scans its parts and forms.

Rhythm is often established by the use of regular repetition. One way to achieve repetition is to replicate whole forms or formal motifs, without regard to their spacing, interval, or placement on or in a building. An example of this is the use of a particular slope on all roof parts and areas of a building; the interval at

which these occur or are perceived to occur need not follow any discernible pattern—the replication of form itself is enough.

The forms of both the walls and the roofs of the apartments shown in figure 5-27 illustrate this concept. Though similar, the repeating forms are not all identical; this results in the base rhythm that is generated by each apartment unit being overlaid with a longer rhythm resulting from the repetition of groups of the units.

Another way to achieve repetition is by interval—the interval between simple forms (whether these are formally or only functionally similar) serves as the thing repeated, and this introduces rhythm.

DOMINANCE/SUBORDINATION

Design decisions about the relative dominance or subordination of various structural components often arise by default out of considerations and decisions about other design variables. This is unfortunate because decisions affecting dominance and subordination can have critical results on overall scale.

In past times, particularly during the period when the accepted educational model for architects was the method of the Beaux Arts, questions of dominance and subordination were almost automatically resolved because of the strong emphasis on symmetry. When the principles of Modern architecture were introduced, the insistence upon symmetry lost some of its force, making independent consideration of dominance and subordination more important.

Obviously, the application of these paired concepts in a particular case is based on the designer's determination as to which parts of a building or assemblage should assume greater and which lesser visual importance. Dominance can be effected by a void, as well as by a physical form—consider, for example, the great reliance on high, arched center openings by many Renaissance architects. Many means are available to the designer for achieving dominance or for determining dominance and subordination; the whole range of principles and elements of scale can and should be brought into the process.

In figure 5–28, we see clearly the dominance of the center tower form, and the subordination of all other parts in this composition—the major roof forms below, the chimney, and even the miniature corner towers.

5–28. Episcopal Church, Asheville, North Carolina.

5—29. Market entrance, Guatemala City.

PRECEDENCE/EMPHASIS

Precedence and emphasis are closely linked to dominance and subordination, but whereas dominance and subordination address the static aspects of form and scale, precedence and emphasis address the dynamic or kinetic aspects of architectural form and scale.

Precedence may introduce, establish, and support the dominant element or elements in a visual composition, but its basis for doing so is time rather than mass or some other static quality. Precedence and emphasis are thus closely related to (and engage) the principles of rhythm and repetition.

Precedence describes what comes first in time, what second, and so on. In other words, it describes a processional, temporal experience. Precedence need not be expressed in an entirely linear way, but per-

fectly valid reasons often exist for controlling a visual/-spatial experience so that the result is linear or sequential. Emphasis takes place along the processional route to provide the processionary modes; it can be created by manipulation of almost any building variable available to the designer.

Two kinds of precedence/emphasis can be seen in figures 5–29 and 5–30. In the first, the strong, processional thrust is clearly expressed. In the second, a subtler and more complex action is underway: the tower (the older part of the construction) establishes precedence in both time and space and sets the theme for the entire assemblage. Then, however, the viewer proceeds visually, if not physically, to the newer and more massive (though also more reserved) sanctuary because the tower as a space is obviously only a small, open pavilion, whereas the larger, lower mass very likely serves as the actual site where the "business" of the establishment takes place.

5–30. First Baptist Church,
Nashville.

5–31. Foreground: One Commerce Place; background: Andrew Jackson State Office Building; Nashville.

5-32. Veterans Administration Hospital, Nashville.

TENSION

Tension here refers to the visual effect of an apparent stress in the relationship of parts, of a lack of equilibrium, or of some other departure from our expectation of a building in repose. Tension is useful in establishing and enhancing precedence and emphasis. It can also be used to develop appropriate areas of dominance and subordination, to manipulate space and spatial experience (perhaps its most common use), and to further many other design goals.

The use of scale-controlling elements, as discussed on page 44, can have the primary or secondary goal of producing tension—the kind of tension that progresses through compression, release, and recompression as a way of generating movement and controlling its pace. Figure 5-31 shows tension of this type developed over a series of buildings. Psychological excitement, even exhilaration, can be generated by such a procession through constricted spaces, culminating in an explosion of openness.

Other kinds of tension exist and can be enlisted by the designer for a multitude of purposes. In figure 5-32, for example, the play of the highly articulated entrance canopy against the rather plain form and detail of the main building produces an interesting outward "pull." The perceptive viewer should also be able to identify other examples of tension in various forms. The use of tension to produce a desired scale or scalar effect may be more difficult than the use of other design elements, but the potential excellence of the results makes such use very attractive.

PROPORTION

Proportion is the relative size, or size in ratio, of two or more elements in a design composition. Often the parts considered in terms of proportion are two opposing dimensions of the same form or space, such as height to width. At its most fundamental level, the concept is easy to understand and is something most of us have recognized in the physical world since childhood. We may not, however, so readily recognize the specific effects proportion has on architectural scale unless the presence of extremes of difference in height to width make them relatively easy to perceive and to assess in terms of fitness.

Proportion has the potential for strong effects on scale—particularly in interior space—when it is combined with other elements, but by itself it can only establish relativities, not anything fixed. At some point, the designer must settle upon an invariable reference dimension of measurable size. Once a governing dimension has been set, a base data line exists, and proportion can then be brought in and used to great advantage in designing for correctness and completeness in scale. Often the base selected is one of the overall plan dimensions, or it may be the floor area in square footage; the choices are governed by economics as much as by anything else. Thereafter, the remaining choices about height, width, and all other unresolved dimensions may and should be made with careful attention to proportion.

Oversimplified methods of gauging dimensions are readily available to the designer. One of the most tempting is reliance on predetermined formulas, which typically have been developed without regard to any particular application or to the unique requirements of a specific design assignment. Chief among these are the various permutations of the golden mean or golden section—a proportional relationship in which the smaller of two perpendicular dimensions relates to the larger in the same way as the larger relates to the sum of the two. Mathematically, the golden mean can be expressed as approximately 1:1.618.

When seen in rectangular form in direct elevation, buildings drawn up in accordance with proportions based on the golden section may indeed strike us as attractive. Figure 5–33 offers a typical example of a traditional approach to church design, yielding expected proportions. The golden mean cannot, however, account for the appearance of the building from different views, it is unable to take special environmental conditions into consideration, and (perhaps worst of all) it represents in every case a failure to undertake fresh, new, unpackaged architecture.

Many theories—some of genuine historical interest, but all flawed to some extent by generality, inaccuracy, or both—have been developed to explain why a well-loved building commands our admiration. Indeed, it is doubtful that the designers of any other historical period could have been as self-conscious as we about such abstract concerns. We must not allow our fascination with theories of proportion (or of anything else) and with formulas derived from them to distract us from addressing each unique architectural project with critical vision, evaluation, and judgment—and all architectural projects are unique. The concept of proportion should serve, not be served; this is the danger of architects' turning in lock-step to predigested answers.

5—33. Hillsboro Church of Christ, Nashville.

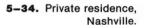

5–34. Private residence, Nashville.

BALANCE/SYMMETRY

In the Beaux Arts tradition, great stress was placed on balance (the general concept) and symmetry (a specific type of balance). There are two basic notions about balance. The first, often termed "symmetrical balance," describes a situation in which two halves of an object divided visually by a (usually) perpendicular plane are perfect or near-perfect mirror images of each other. The second, sometimes called "dynamic balance," describes an approximately equal summing up of the elements on either side of a readily perceived visual fulcrum in a building's composition. This has frequently been illustrated by drawing a parallel to the principle of physics according to which unequal lengths of lever arms pivoting on a central fulcrum are held in balance by compensating unequal weights; the analogy is helpful, but of course the actual complexity of form and detail in architecture cannot adequately be represented by a board, a fulcrum, and two lumps of mass.

Balance may or may not in a specific instance have much to do with scale. If it does, its purpose is to provide a foundation of fitness upon which the total assemblage rests, producing the feelings of security and equanimity necessary for appropriate scale.

Figures 5–34 and 5–35 show domestic and heroic examples, respectively, of symmetrical balance. For examples of dynamic balance, see figures 1–6, 7–12, and 8–3. Figure 1–6 shows a handsomely composed small modern office building, though perhaps lacking sufficient small-scale detail; figure 7–12 shows a well-thought-out early twentieth-century firehouse, and figure 8–3 shows a noted Italian cathedral in which the tower serves admirably as a fulcrum. In comparison, figure 6–11 shows a building in which the designer, while providing a symmetrical porch, has (in the name of function) allowed the entryway to be placed awkwardly off-center and has allowed the non-symmetrical sign to dominate the entire front view. This haphazard combination results in a finished facade lacking in balance, unsettling in aspect, and unresolved in scale.

5–35. St. Mary's Cathedral,
San Francisco.

VARIETY/UNITY

In whole and integrated architectural design, unity is a highly desirable goal, but it should not be obtained at the expense of variety: unity requires neither dullness nor uniformity.

Variety can be asserted in many ways and at many different levels of choice in the design process. The unifying device, though, is a single design concept, around which variety is clustered or draped in a

5–36. Rutledge Hill, Nashville.

way that neither obscures nor damages the central unity.

Means of introducing unifying devices include: using the same type or size of windows throughout a building; using the same roof slope on all roof parts; and using specific materials in the same ways throughout the building. All of these and more can be seen in figure 5–36. These late nineteenth-century town houses show an exuberance of detail, even though as examples they are relatively restrained for the era and type.

The variety/unity concept may be the most fundamental of all elements and principles in achieving a desired scale in our designs. If we can accept the premise that variety represents the entire array of individual concepts discussed in this chapter, then it becomes exceedingly important in achieving good scale to understand the notion of unity as representing the essential ideas of wholeness and fitness.

Intellectual pondering in our field is useful only to a point; to be tested, ideas must be "realized," and this happens when we move on from our pondering to our real work—forming images with our hands, judging them with our eyes, testing them with our intellects, and animating them with our spirits.

My hope in reintroducing the elements and principles discussed above in light of what may be a fresh appreciation of scale is that they will become a part of the designer's consciousness during the design process, and that eventually, after much practice with them, the designer can assimilate them into an active intuition capable of informing every product with a powerful and unified expression.

6. Parameters of Scale

Whereas the words "elements and principles" have been used to designate the basic conceptual options available to the designer, the term "parameters" is used here to identify some of the more fundamental ways in which these options may be used. While elements and principles represent the designer's tools, parameters are the ways they can be used.

DISTANCE

One of the most apparent and comprehensible of the parameters of scale is distance. The distance from which we view a building directly affects our perception of the whole and of its scale. Of course, our perception can be quite different from the strict facts about the object we view. The disappearance of any visible pattern in brickwork when we stand a sufficient distance from it is an example of the distance phenomenon. We see the same brick wall at two, twenty, two hundred, and (perhaps) two thousand feet, but it will appear different to us and will give us a different body of data about itself at each of these distances.

A brick wall inherently has the capacity to communicate different but complementary sets of information about itself at different distances. Other kinds of walls may do this less well, or perhaps not at all.

As we approach a building from a great distance, the increasing resolution of what is perceived gives us satisfaction in its progressive revelation; it intrigues us at the same time as, by stages, it reveals itself. The view possible at the greatest distance (unless obscured by other objects in the surroundings) takes in the building's entire form and mass. The precise appearance of the form and mass changes, of course, depending on the particular direction of approach to be taken, but at great distances variations in direction of approach reveal little additional detail. As we move toward the building and reach intermediate distances, the consequences are mixed: our perceptions of form and mass become progressively more strained and difficult, but more and more detail becomes apparent. When we have arrived very close to the building, its overall form and mass are not very clear since so little of it can be seen; but the small, intimate detail is readily perceived and understood.

Figures 6–1 through 6–3 show three views of the same building at three different distances along essentially the same line of approach, illustrating the different kinds of information communicated at these distances when balanced range of scale is present.

The perceived scale of a building is therefore in one respect a function of distance. If the perceived scale seems distorted or differs from our expectations, the building can be described as having poor scale or as being out of scale. This applies to a building that, when seen from a distance, projects an incorrect statement of its actual size. Many public buildings, including some that are quite well known, possess this

6–1. Life and Casualty Tower, Nashville.

6–2. Life and Casualty Tower, Nashville.

6–3. Life and Casualty Tower, Nashville.

quality of misrepresentation. It is discussed in a very telling and thorough manner by Brent C. Brolin in his book *The Failure of Modern Architecture.* *

Many Modern buildings present such a limited range of scale that they have no distance distinctiveness—that is, the buildings reveal the same amount and kind of information about themselves from every distance. This can be seen perhaps most readily in the typical glass-skin curtain-wall type of building enclosure. Commonly, we cannot even determine where the floors are in such buildings except at night when the lights come on. The message projected then is extremely different from that transmitted in the daytime.

* New York: Van Nostrand Reinhold Company, 1976.

6–4. Life and Casualty Tower, Nashville.

ASPECT

Aspect is a parameter based on the direction from which a person views and/or approaches a construction. Both distance and aspect relate to the changes in our perception over time as we change our viewing position—by moving closer or farther away in the first case, and by moving around the object in the other. Changes in the way a building looks to us from different viewing positions occur not only because of concrete differences in the form and detail that are visible but also because of differing natural and humanly imposed conditions that govern the quantity and type of light falling upon or emanating from the building. While two or more sides of a building may be nearly identical, our perception of them will not be so because natural light never falls the same way on surfaces facing different directions; even overcast skies rarely confound entirely our sense of the sun's orientation.

Figures 6–4 and 6–5 show two more views of the same building presented in figures 6–1 through 6–3—ground-level views from different angles at approximately the same distance from the building. The differing information made available as the viewing aspect changes is very obvious here.

6–5. Life and Casualty Tower, Nashville.

TIME

In addition to its application to the concepts of distance and aspect, the notion of time can be considered as an independent parameter of scale. Because of the nature of sunlight, changes in our perception of a building occur over time without there being any changes in the building's physical condition or our viewing position.

Different amounts and kinds of information about the building are revealed to us under different temporal conditions; and if the building has been designed with appropriate attention to scale, all of the many views presented under these conditions will add to our knowledge and understanding of the building's size and scale. The breadth of change attributable to the parameter of time can readily be seen in figures 6–6 and 6–7, in which the same building is shown at dawn and mid-afternoon.

6—7. Late afternoon, Green Hills Post Office, Nashville.

RANGE OF SCALE

Buildings (and other objects of similar size) consist of elements drawn from a broad range of comprehensible sizes—from the smallest discernible unit to the whole building. Their range of scale is good (or balanced) when elements of all sizes have been developed with the same degree of attention and care.

A doorknob is a good example of an element close to the small end of this elemental spectrum. It is a very familiar and useful object, one whose forms communicate to us in personal and direct terms. To function, it must satisfy a narrowly prescribed size relationship to a very special part of the human body, the hand. At the opposite end of the spectrum, obviously, is the entire building.

When the designer's attention to form is concentrated at one end of the range of scale, the character of the whole is affected, and a specialized visual effect, or demeanor, is produced. Concentrating attention on larger elements at the expense of smaller ones tends to make a building appear monumental. This occurs because emphasizing elements that are large in relation to the human body encourages us to feel less significant and therefore overpowered by them.

In figure 6–8, we see a close-up view of Nashville's re-creation of the Parthenon—a building originally conceived and built to overwhelm people

6–8. The Parthenon, Nashville.

6—9. Immanuel Baptist Church, Nashville.

for religious purposes; notice the double-scaled steps of the podium, making intermediate steps necessary at the point of actual entry. The building in figure 6–9 shows a recent reinterpretation of the Doric idiom, wherein the extreme simplification of form and the removal of almost all small detail have contributed to a feeling of monumentality in a very small structure.

On the other hand, concentrating attention on the smaller elements at the expense of the larger tends to make a building seem diminutive or intimate. By concentrating attention on such small elements as window muntins, porch and rooftop railings, brick

quoins, and slim, paired columns, the building in figure 6–10 exhibits the characteristics of intimacy or diminutiveness, apparently as a result of conscious design effort. The building shown in figure 6–11, on the other hand, possesses a seemingly inadvertent (and certainly unintegrated) conjunction of monumental and diminutive forms, although it is true that many of the same smaller elements have been emphasized here as in figure 6–10.

Dominating a building with elements that tend toward either extreme will produce one of the above effects in design and scale. If this is the designer's aim,

6—10. Daisy's Restaurant, Nashville.

6—11. The Game Room, Nashville.

well and good; but I suspect that, in many of the buildings exhibiting a predominant monumentality or diminutiveness, these effects were produced by default (and with a marked insensitivity to range of scale) rather than by design. A building that shows a balanced range of scale will seem more integrated, more in harmony with itself and with its environment than most monumental or diminutive constructions do.

A number of builders and architects throughout history give evidence of having understood the concept of range of scale. In accordance with their understanding, they have manipulated building forms in order to influence people and achieve other ends. Consider how many monumental-scaled buildings have been erected by princes of state, church, and commerce, with the goal of establishing and maintaining power over people. Of course, the manipulation of range of scale may be thought a benign, honorable, or aesthetically appropriate activity in any particular case: the parameter itself carries no moral weight.

Too often designers working in the Modern idiom base decisions affecting the detail of form on narrowly conceived rationales that have unfortunate and unwanted secondary effects on scale. This has resulted in buildings that, by their ignorance of range of scale, seem gross or dull or pompous or dainty or fussy or some hybrid of these traits.

A NOTE ON ORNAMENT

In 1892, Louis Sullivan commented that, for him, the purpose of ornament was to enrich and flesh out the basic mass and form of good architecture. He thought that plant forms provided the most appropriate inspiration for ornament, perhaps because he felt ornament should emerge from the structure, basic form, and mass of a building in the same organic way that plants grow out of and into their environments.

During the later years of the Modern era, ornament came to be looked upon with disdain and sometimes disparagement. Many buildings were stripped of all signs of tradition: architectural amnesiacs were produced—both buildings and designers. Most architects, however, continued to appreciate the valuable visual and emotional functions ornament had traditionally served, and they sought to reenlist through the use of other elements some of those functions. In Mies's Barcelona Pavilion, for example, the crisp, hard edges of the forms, the grain of the marble, and the reflections in the chrome and other high-gloss surfaces provide the visual and emotional enrichment that ornament might have provided in earlier days.

Ornament should not be attached to buildings in the manner of unrelated decorations. Its form and function should grow out of the underlying structure of the building as Sullivan thought; furthermore, ornament can go beyond Sullivan's concept to include service to the fully developed concept of scale. The use of ornament to improve and complete scale in buildings may thus be seen as an expression of Sullivan's concepts combined with the tenets of the more recent Modern masters, in whose hands ornamental functions are performed by the basic fabric of the building rather than by applied trimming.

Just because we include in a building design a feature that is instantly recognizable as ornament does not mean it will improve the scale of the building. A recent, highly publicized twelve-story building features huge, stylized garlands strung between floors at about the seventh/eighth floor level. These are so large and shallow that they appear to be painted on—and might as well be for the effect they have. In fact, they only distort scale, making the rather fat, squat mass of the building seem even fatter and squatter.

The lesson to be learned is that a complementary consistency must be maintained in the scale of the ornament and of the entire building. If this can be mastered, the designer will have gained another tool to use in directing the various parameters that animate design and in making the resulting architecture touch and speak to people more completely and more satisfyingly.

7. Learning from What We Find around Us

Much can be learned about applying scale by studying almost any building. The other major part of the process of learning how to apply our knowledge of scale consists of practice.

These are the kinds of questions we need to ask continually about any building we are studying, as well as about any we are in the process of designing:

- Do its major proportions appear to be in correct harmony?

- Do the major parts, elements, and features stand on their own *and* in proper subordination to the whole? to the secondary and tertiary features?

- Do building elements communicate appropriate information (both in terms of amount and of quality) at different viewing distances?

- Is there distinct resolution where the walls meet the ground plane? How has this been accomplished?

- Are features relating the structure to human dimensions present and understandable? Do these relate to full figures? the hand? the height above ground level of a standing person's hand? a step or tread?

- Do any surfaces visually invite touching? stroking? gripping?

- How have textures been used, and what do they do for scale?

- Is the range of scale weighted toward either end of the spectrum, or is it evenly distributed? How do people respond to this condition? Does it suit the nature and purpose of the building?

The importance and value of these questions are to be found in the process of examination. After analyzing in this way a fairly extensive sampling of buildings of several sizes and types, an observer should begin to get a feeling for how buildings work and do not work. The habit of examining with this kind of critical eye the buildings and other built objects we see around us every day is one kind of practice—a kind that will undergird our confidence in our future design work.

ARCHITECTURAL TRADITIONS

Much can also be learned from looking at the specifics of particular traditional styles. Classical architecture—some of whose features we have already discussed—represents one of three primary strains of traditional architecture found in the United States, the other two being Hispanic and Gothic. The importance of these somewhat arbitrary categories lies not particularly in where the architectural types they represent actually originated, but rather in what ex-

isted in the places and times that witnessed the adoption of the particular characteristics of each.

Aside from economic, religious, and other cultural considerations, climate probably has been the most important of the determinants—in many cases overshadowing all others. For this reason locales of similar climate in totally different parts of the world sometimes produce very similar results in the features of buildings. The arid regions of Central America and North Africa have much in common, for example, and the remarkable similarities of the independently originated Hispanic and North African architectural types can provide the inquiring designer with a firm idea of invariable needs of architecture in particular climatic settings.

The purpose, then, of the categories discussed below is not to make claims of historical precision and accuracy but rather to identify in a simple fashion certain clusters of architectural consistancies—clustering them only to learn from them for future applications.

GRECO-ROMAN

Many of the features of Greco-Roman or Classical architecture were appropriated and incorporated into later historical styles. In the first-century Roman theater at Leptis Magna, (in present-day Libya) seen in figure 7–1, we see the richness possible in the Greco-Roman vocabulary. The Athenian Parthenon can be seen in figures 7–2 and 7–3. The first shows the original in its present state of ruin; the second the early twentieth-century re-creation built in Nashville. As a final example of the Greco-Roman strain, figure 7–4 shows a typical twentieth-century church that features simplified classical motifs.

7–1. First-century Roman Theater, Leptis Magna, Libya.

7–2. The Parthenon, Athens (original).

7–3. The Parthenon, Nashville (recreation).

7–4. Belmont United Methodist Church, Nashville.

Not only in Renaissance Italy but also in Federalist America, Classicism was promoted as a suitable form of social and political expression, and as a result this strain received new boosts in popularity at those points along the continuum of time, propelled by political forces.

7—5. China Art Center, Carmel, California.

HISPANIC

Hispanic, as used here, includes both European and indigenous American features: the lavishness of Baroque Spanish colonial and the simplicity of Pueblo adobe, as well as everything the melding of European and native cultures has produced.

The forms, features, and special attributes of the Hispanic strain arose in large measure as appropriate responses to a climate with special characteristics—bright, hard sunshine, little rain, low humidity, and few overcast days. They also arose in response to locally available building materials, to existing technology, and to the values, aspirations, vision, and vigor of the people. None of these can be discounted; all contributed to Hispanic architecture's richness and range of expression.

Nonetheless, as valuable as an understanding of these aspects can be generally, their value specifically to the study of scale is minimal and should be con-sidered subordinate to an understanding of the structures that were produced and of the messages and teachings these communicate to us today.

The great variety found within the Hispanic category can be seen in figures 7–5 through 7–8. Figure 7–5 shows a detail of a typical building from the American Southwest. The next two are of residences of similar size, both from Guatemala City, but the products of different historical periods: the building in figure 7–6 is from the nineteenth century; the one in figure 7–7 is from the 1980s. Figure 7–8 shows a recent Central American church, reconstructed after a 1976 earthquake in close resemblance to the eighteenth-century original. The scene in figure 7–9 is from Mediterranean North Africa, whose climate is similar to that of the unforested parts of Guatemala; notice the similarity of the response to climatic conditions—relatively small openings in unbroken areas of thick wall, elaborate railings and grillework, light colors, flat roof decks, and so forth.

7-6. Older private residence, Guatemala City.

7-7. Recent private residence, Guatemala City.

LEARNING FROM WHAT WE FIND AROUND US 89

7–8. Church, Guatemala City.

7—9.
Street scene,
Tripoli, Libya.

GOTHIC AND AMERICAN GOTHIC

The Gothic strain in American architecture arrived here from a cold, cloud-covered Northern European landscape—an environment not unlike that found in large sections of North America, showing the impetus for American Gothic to be not only religion-based, but also climate-based.

During the nineteenth century, architectural revivalism became very popular in the United States, culminating near the end of the century in an exuberant amalgamation of sundry styles that was termed "eclecticism." Classical features, Gothic features, even Egyptian features (see figure 4–9)—promoted by the popular interest in contemporaneous archeological discoveries in Egypt—were brought together in what seems to us now a quaint and even outlandish disarray. Nonetheless, the products of this movement often exhibited great vigor and a remarkable feeling for scale. In fact, the very lack of restraint in combining disparate traditional style signatures produced a discipline of its own. For convenience and because it so typifies the vigor of the late nineteenth century, I would place Richardsonian Romanesque architecture under the heading American Gothic.

Obviously, our inventory of American buildings contains no examples of first-generation Gothic. Our transplanted versions come from the revival and eclectic periods and hence are reinterpretations, filtered through the intervening time and culture of those periods. Under the Gothic umbrella, a large range of expressions, interpretations, and applications can be found—from nearly perfect copies of cathedrals to half-timbered replicas of Tudor cottages.

We can see by comparing figures 7–10 and 7–11 the similarities between the original, and the descendant, transferred to American soil, as well as distinctive, though subtle, differences. In figures 7–12 and 7–13 two more examples of American adaptation of the original Gothic vocabulary are shown, the first a firehouse and the second a residence—both from the early twentieth century.

7–10. Amiens Cathedral, Amiens, France.

7–11. United States Customs House, Nashville.

7–12. Hillsboro Road Fire Station, Nashville.

7–13. Private residence in the Tudor style, Nashville.

94 SCALE IN ARCHITECTURE

EVALUATING HISTORICAL ARCHITECTURE

On the most elementary level, the designers and builders of the structures from which we deduce Classical, Hispanic, and Gothic architecture handled their assignments with remarkable sensitivity to the issues of human scale. The limitations of their particular architectural vocabularies and of the societies and economies that supported them were treated as bases for disciplined creativity rather than as excuses for mindless repetition of preexisting work.

In analyzing historic styles, we should attempt to evaluate not only how specific issues—the elements, principles, and parameters discussed in previous chapters—were addressed, but also how various responses to these issues have been integrated successfully in individual buildings. Because it is possible for a designer to get all the detail right and still lose sight of the overall objective of producing architecture, we must ask in each case whether the building we are studying succeeds as a unified work of architecture.

INTERIOR SPACE

Both in detail and in proportions, much remains to be learned from past uses of interior space. After several decades during which little architectural interest was shown in them, large, highly articulated interior spaces are now enjoying renewed popularity.

One important contributor to this trend has been the rediscovery of the central atrium, first in designs for hotels and shopping malls, and more recently in designs for office buildings and even schools. These are essentially expanded and elaborated circulation spaces, although their adaptability to a range of scalar functions enables them to take on a highly individual life of their own.

The other major type of interior space, somewhat less frequently used in recent construction than the atrium, is the terminal or destination space. Examples include assembly spaces such as theaters, concert halls, church sanctuaries, other auditoriums, and indoor sports arenas (generally the largest spaces in both seating capacity and sheer volume).

To say that all major interior spaces fall into one of these two basic types, although generally true, may be misleading because they can have a great variety of functions and meanings for us. A single space can serve for both circulation and destination, in addition to signifying other things to us in groups and as individuals. In judging a space, we must ask how well its scale supports these functions and meanings.

The interior views shown in figures 7–14 through 7–17 provide a wide spectrum of details and features, and reveal an equally wide range of historical forms and attitudes. The interior space of the Spanish Gothic Toledo Cathedral (figure 7–14), serves both for circulation and as terminus. The magnificent Moorish courtyard in figure 7–15, though technically outdoors, provides an excellent model for handling interior space because of its well-developed air of internal fitness.

If we compare the details of the modern church shown in figure 5–9 with those of the Toledo Cathedral, we can see how the design decisions faced in each were resolved in ways that express not only the historical period involved, but also the designer's sensitivity to scale and human values. Figures 7–16 and 7–17

7–14. Toledo Cathedral,
Toledo, Spain.

7–16. Belmont Mansion, Nashville.

show two interior spaces that are similar in actual size but come from different American historical periods, the first from the antebellum South and the second from the 1960s. Notice how in figure 7–17 the features of wood paneling, ceiling beams, floor pattern, and fireplace all give scalar clues.

The quality of height should be considered in an interior space. Some practical uses of a space—for example, sports such as basketball, volleyball, and gymnastics—impose height requirements on it. Tiered seating created to provide good sight lines for desired seating capacity may also impose height requirements for the space. Other uses may impose height requirements for aesthetic or spiritual reasons. Churches, for example, often justify ceiling heights that go beyond any practical requirement of seating or acoustics, on grounds of theological expression or symbolism.

The quality of height in a large interior space (as well as quantitative factors of pure physical dimensions and proportions) is an essential part of the overall experience a building offers its occupants. The qualitative nature of the overhead space includes such features as its shape (flat, domed, arched, and so on), color, texture, articulation, and use of light.

As height increases, different and more complex transitional features may become desirable. One frequent mistake on the part of designers is to imagine that in instances of dealing with severe vertical space, such as in a hotel atrium, they may treat the walls uniformly all the way up to the ceiling—perhaps twenty stories away. Unfortunately, such uniformity of treatment can have the effect of making viewers looking up from the main floor feel as though they are standing at the bottom of a silo—an uncomfortable

feeling for most people. This kind of feeling could be avoided by varying the way the wall is treated at different heights.

In some spaces such as gymnasiums, high quality finishes are generally considered unjustified; pipes, conduits, ducts, and other utilitarian elements are frequently left exposed above our heads in these spaces, where we are not expected to look anyway. Most spectators, however, seek, visual and even physical relief from the tense atmosphere of a sports contest by looking upward or around the arena, and may wish at such moments that the designer and the owner had provided more than pipes and trusses as a backdrop. Nevertheless, in the absence of more thoughtfully provided features, these purely functional elements can communicate a sense of scale to us.

Even in the bare-bones space of a school gymnasium, the structural realities—bleachers, goals, ventilators, and so on—can be enlisted to help answer the viewers' questions of scale. A wise and sometimes witty designer working with a miserly budget may still be able to produce a little gem in a big gym.

In interiors, no less than on building exteriors, the edge where wall meets floor presents a critical and often overlooked design issue. We tend to look at a wall kinetically at our eye-height, moving our eyes either up or down. What we see at the wall's terminus or edge tells us much about scale. In moving our eyes down toward the floor, we tend to go rapidly, especially if the wall surface is uniform and monolithic. We need a transition—a device for slowing our eye movement down before it visually slams into the floor.

This is the primary scalar rationale for providing a baseboard of some sort (although baseboards also

7-17. Cravens Hall, The University of the South, Sewanee, Tennessee.

serve the practical purpose of covering up the raw edges of the wall and floor materials). Visually, we need the subtlety and softening of a more gradual transition. Almost without exception, simply setting a baseboard against the wall-floor edge helps to tie down the scale of the space.

The junction of wall and ceiling involves a somewhat different set of requirements. We tend to approach this edge from an angle of view that is more acute than the angle from which we look at the baseboard. The cornice, or its equivalent, will probably be actually and observably out of reach (unlike the baseboard), and therefore will have a different scalar message for us.

Traditionally, crown molds and their variants have fulfilled these and other visual needs where wall and ceiling meet. Moldings, devices, and features of other types in traditional architecture, such as trim around doors and other openings or trim applied to planar and articulated surfaces, provided accent, focus, and balance to interior spaces. When Modern architecture abandoned these features, designs were often left adrift without scale-giving anchors in a trackless sea of monotonous surface uniformity.

A few sensitive architects have been able to create successful and satisfying spaces by focusing on the abstract qualities of sculptural space itself and thereby minimizing the impact of detail. Many architects working in this vein, however, have simply adopted some form of the seductive and facile formula of minimalism. Still other architects have incorporated elements drawn directly from historical forms, but have removed them from the contextual relationships in which they originated, causing distortion of the sense of scale the forms traditionally offered to viewers and users.

In designing interior spaces, our intention should be to restore a sense of scale through devices of our own choosing, our own invention, our own time. We can use concepts from the past without using forms from the past; we can and should use the eternals of architecture—for example, the fact that enclosures and the materials used in them must have certain physical characteristics such as color, texture, shape, and edge.

PARALLELS AND ANALOGIES

From time to time over recent history, observers have found parallels and analogies by which to relate architecture to other scholarly disciplines or natural orders. The examination of some of these analogies may help us in our quest for learning from the buildings we find around us. If we can look at our surroundings and our activities in fresh and open ways, our capacity for learning should be enhanced and enlarged, and our ability to understand scale and incorporate it into our designs should be enriched.

Goethe spoke of architecture as "frozen music." This is an intriguing notion: what parallels to music can be found in architecture?

One of the most basic must be the concept of "form and content." In music (as in other forms of "literature"), form describes the overall or basic structure. Content refers to the nuances of orchestration—of coloration, phrasing, meter, and the specific key or keys. A single popular ballad can be rendered dozens of different ways by as many artists. The basic structure or form of the sequence of notes and intervals of time between each is the same for the same song, but vastly different results are possible by means of differences in content.

Some productions (recordings, primarily) are the work of a single performer accompanying himself or herself on guitar or piano. Most, though, are the result of the combined talents of scores of artists and technicians. These people rarely do their various jobs simultaneously and at a single locale, even if the end product is made to sound as if it were spontaneously produced in a single sitting from beginning to end.

In architecture, many buildings share very similar forms—simple rectilinear boxes, gabled roof shapes, and single-sloped sheds, for example. The range of simple forms is fairly narrow and the first major step in elaboration is the combination of separate construction masses into clusters. Even so, many buildings are little distinct from their neighbors until they reach the level of detail, surface treatment, solid and void, ornamentation, and color, which taken collectively may be described as the content level of the building. The architectural elements in this concept of content often have direct musical parallels—color/ coloration, rhythm/meter, dominance/accent, and so forth.

As is true with any analogy, the implications of this one can be disputed at various points. The idea of "frozen music" may be at fault in suggesting an essentially static quality in architecture because, even though it usually stands still (or is supposed to!), a great deal of lively, soul-satisfying movement can be experienced in architecture. In Gothic cathedrals, movement is so powerfully present that all are con-

scious of it. The phrase, "soaring vaults" arises subconsciously and speaks to us in a readily understood way. We sense that the entire structure is held in dynamic tension even if we can not rationally explain why.

Movement can also travel through architecture in a processional manner, by means of repetitions, sequential presentations of elements, or other rhythm-inducing designs. Finally, our eye's constant scanning of our natural and built environments constitutes another form of movement—a free movement within the basic controlled movement pattern in and around architecture—which might be compared with musical improvisation in jazz and certain other musical types, or to Marshall McLuhan's notion of "subjective completion."

Other musical parallels can doubtless be found, but perhaps the most important thing to recognize is that architecture possesses the dual qualities of form and content. The discovery and understanding of form and content in a particular design commission may lead the architect to a higher plane of architecture than might otherwise be achieved.

Another easily grasped analogy is in the area of human physiology: architecture requires systems for structure (a skeleton), enclosure (skin), ventilation (lungs), energy conversion (the digestive system), plumbing (the bloodstream), electrical power (muscles), controls (nerves), and so on. Such comparisons can suggest new ways of understanding the relationships among these systems in architecture, the roles the various systems play, and their potential impact on design.

A third analogy can be comprehended between a

building and a community or an ecological system. In this analogy, the roles of a building in the larger community of buildings and in the rest of the surrounding environment may be seen as parallels to analogous roles of a human being in the natural world. What function does the building perform in the society of its peers? What is its effect on and relationship to the larger environment? How can we design our buildings to address responsibly these functions, effects, and relationships?

Le Corbusier called his kind of architecture a "machine for living." This is becoming increasingly appropriate as technology progresses and as we make buildings that more and more closely resemble machines. Likewise, at the same time as we are making machines seem more human (interactive video games and home computers, for example), we are also making machines seem more buildinglike. The computerization of our automobiles and major appliances is approaching the level of the centralized systems we have come to expect in buildings. The term "architecture" has even been appropriated by the computer industry! Buildings really can be seen as machines of a special sort—ones that (usually) must interact with and accomodate within themselves human activity, ones whose roles include dealing with the external forces of nature.

A machine, though, is fundamentally a technological creation conceived and evaluated on a purely scientific basis. While it may be styled to be more visually attractive or marketable, a machine's functions (its work and, therefore, its value) depend for their justification on purely objective utilitarian grounds. Architecture, on the other hand, while it must satisfy many scientifically based criteria, must first satisfy subjective human demands for function, work, and value, and its success in doing so can ultimately be evaluated only by subjection to the entire range of human thought, from rational to intuitive. This is the range of evaluation expressed in Vitruvius's standard: "firmness, commodity, and delight."

A final area of comparison involves language as an analogy to architecture. Sometimes called "semiotics" (the study of signs, symbols, and their meaning), it has generated much commentary but unfortunately little consensus among its proponents. Some writers have focused on the concept of grammatical structure (or syntax) and parts of speech as analogies to architectural counterparts. Others have attempted to discover meanings in architecture and in specific buildings in structures paralleling those by which meaning is conveyed in language.

This may be seen by some as straining too hard to find sheep among the clouds. Still, there may be value in the effort, and for us to ignore the possibility of communication from and with architecture would be to miss a great opportunity to improve our ability to enjoy and to produce architecture at new and richer levels.

Any mental activity of which human beings are capable, so long as it is directed toward noble ends, should be welcomed for the contribution it potentially makes to mankind's collective wisdom. This certainly includes analogies and parallels such as those mentioned here.

8. Summing Up

In the mid-1970s, a neighborhood citizen's organization in Nashville sponsored a charette, involving teams of students from several universities in the region, to generate and develop land-use alternatives to a proposed interstate highway connector loop that was about to be constructed through its territory. At the final public presentation meeting, the featured speaker was Edmund Bacon, the noted city planner and author (*Design of Cities*). Being a meeting of neighborhood activists, people of all ages were in attendance, including entire families. In the middle of Bacon's talk, a four-year-old girl strolled across the front of the room, directly in front of Bacon. He stopped and, pointing to the child, said that it was she—not any of us of older generations—whom we all ought to be designing for.

Whom are we designing for? And for what kind of world?

Changes in virtually every aspect of public and private life are occurring, with seemingly ever-increasing speed. We are often told that we are moving from the industrial age toward the electronic age or from a manufacturing economy to an economy based on communications, and that this is having and will have momentous effects on the workplace and on private life. We hear reports that Western society is becoming more decentralized, and we are informed and warned about innumerable other changes, actual and foretold.

What impact will these have on architecture? It is easy to spot and evaluate some effects in areas of architectural practice, but understanding their meaning for architecture itself—the product of that practice—will be considerably more difficult.

The integration of scalar design into a personal philosophy of design and practice will not, of course, make that understanding any easier to attain. However, once understanding and assimilation have been reached, we should feel encouraged to deal with future realities in a more responsible and confident way.

Scale is a tricky subject, one abundant both in opportunities for enlightened, enhanced design and in potential pitfalls of triteness.

In the building shown in figure 8–1, the rail on the roof (being only about two feet high) makes the eaves seem much farther away from us than they really are, and therefore makes the building appear taller and more imposing than it really is. The ironwork rails at the balconies give a true scale reading. Notice too that the eave-line rail is heavy and articulated in dimension and is painted white, which makes it more visually prominent, while the balcony rails are thin, regular bars painted a dark color. They almost disappear against the dark background.

I seriously doubt that the designer of this building thought about these ideas. However, the design succeeds in giving us a choice example of the manipulative use of scale. The question this raises is whether an architect should or should not choose to use scale in a manipulative way. Designing buildings always in-

8–1. Claridge Condominiums, Nashville.

volves making arbitrary choices; we simply cannot escape them because we have no formula at once so broad and so finely wrought as to tell us the right thing to do at every turn. Designers *must* exercise personal judgment in ways that control the effect their design choices have on scale.

Figure 4–4 provides an example. The height of the parapet on the one-story wing in the center of the picture was certainly an arbitrary choice, as was the choice to have or not to have a parapet. The choice of the height of the parapet was made on the basis of a judgment about proportions, not only of the frontal plane of this wing but also of this element in comparison to others in the assemblage seen from this direction. Visually, this element serves as a link between the large mass of the sanctuary in the background and a smaller but similarly-shaped chapel off-view to the left (see figure 4–1). The designer judged that to form this kind of link the wing needed a certain minimum mass; by using the device of a parapet, the necessary mass was attained. Other project constraints precluded the option of placing the roof plane at this height.

In most instances, the scale and scalar qualities of a building depend on a complex combination of interacting features. Innumerable sources can supply design ideas, many times in unrecognized guises. Good designers may not know why they make particular choices, but by trusting their own sensitivity and insight, they allow wisdom to prevail, so that successful designs result.

A good or adequate design can be enhanced and lifted to unexpected levels of quality by appropriate choices. For example, the building seen in figure 8–2 features a rather wide range of geometric forms in its major parts. Through the judicious choice of a few materials, each (as has been previously noted) giving its own set of scalar values, the assemblage is admirably drawn together in an easily-discernible expression of fitness. The massing, forms, and different textures all work together to produce a truer image of scale than any could do separately.

Design can be enriched by the combination of varied concepts of scale and by the transformation of a strong and clear scalar feature into a general design motif. Such expression is found in the Cathedral of Siena (figure 8–3), whose designer took a very practical functional requirement—the steps, which extend

8–2. Episcopal Church, Asheville, North Carolina.

8—3. Siena Cathedral, Siena, Italy.

around three sides of the podium on which the cathedral sits—and used the idea of horizontal striations suggested by the steps as the basis for a design motif. The overlaying of these stripes makes exceptional an otherwise nicely proportioned but unremarkable Italian Gothic cathedral. The motif introduces rhythm, working in counterpoint to the basic Gothic idea of verticality, and to the fairly orthodox Gothic articulation of the front (which was added later). The combination of the two ideas in one building, while perhaps seeming vaguely unresolved, manages to produce a whole with a greater range of scale and a greater potential for communication than we usually find.*

Looking back into the past, we can see from our vantage point that some values in architecture are enduring and can transcend changes in society and cul-

*As an aside, I wonder if the horizontal bands could have been the progenitor of the heavily rusticated treatment of ground floor exterior walls found in Italian Renaissance palazzi, 200 to 400 years later.

ture—including changes as substantial as those we are witnessing today. What we should be doing, then, is seeking to claim for our own time and our own use values that will endure through changing times and that will continue to speak to people, enriching and affirming their lives. Scale is unquestionably prominent and important among those enduring values.

Design is the heart and soul of architecture, the engine that drives a practice. No matter what else a practice may be or do, it constantly makes statements about design. The people who have final authority over the direction and actuation of a practice determine the role of design in a given project through every decision they make, even if the decision is simply to ignore design.

People can be found who (taken as a group) are able to do a better job than the architect is capable of doing at almost everything the architect does. The only unique and exclusive thing the architect really has to offer, then, is design. It follows that the architect who forgets or ignores design may not actually be practicing architecture at all, but only a form of building-plan space allocation.

Designers need to grow. The product of a particular practice needs to show over time a maturing process and a constantly expanding vocabulary and vision—not as a sign of a restless pursuit of originality (one of those qualities that is never achieved when consciously sought), but as a by-product of a greater search for a continually more unified, enriching, and complete expression in design.

Design (and not necessarily the kind that wins design awards) makes the difference; and by this I mean design that serves society best, making the greatest impact for the benefit of the particular client *and* the whole public. The responsible practitioner should always ask, "Is this the best we can do?" and, "Is this better than we were doing ten years ago or last year?"

An architect need not be a design leader to be a responsible design practitioner, but an architect must have the ability to avoid self-deception, to maintain integrity, and to grow. The specific and general requirements of each particular commission must be satisfied, but a good architect must be willing to go beyond this and must devote more thought, more spirit and more plain hard work to each project than the contract requires.

Responsible architects always seek to understand their clients' value systems and to respect the power and importance that symbols have in society; they always undertake to use and interpret value systems and symbols meaningfully in their designs. A common but avoidable trap for designers is to trivialize symbols and values by insensitive, literal copying. It is each generation's task to reinterpret the past, and this is as true in architecture as in any other field. Such reinterpretation offers the opportunity to restudy questions of scale and to reintegrate scale into building design.

Contrasting examples of interpretation can be seen in figures 5–33 and 8–4. Figure 5–33 shows an instance of the kind of authentic or "correct" copying of detail that ceased to evolve around the time of Christopher Wren, while straying far from the historic model in proportions. The symbolism, rendered in forms originally derived from pagan temples, nonetheless retains great value to people in modern-day religious architectural expression. On the other hand,

8—4. First Baptist Church, Nashville.

the building seen in figure 8–4 reinterprets religious architectural symbols originally generated for the Christian faith in the Middle Ages, and presents two renditions: one from the Victorian era (the tower) and the other from the mid-twentieth century (the sanctuary)—some eighty years apart in execution but palpably from the same family of symbolism.

History and historical form, however, need not be the primary generators of design. Scale can and should form a part of truly original design, just as it should form a part of designs more or less obviously derived from past forms; it is in any case rare to find a new building that is not descended in some way from earlier formal ideas.

I will close with a list of informal rules—reminders, really—for architects and designers:

- Architects must determine, as diligently as they determine functional and programmatic needs, the needs of focus and flow in the space. What are the requirements of focus and how can scale enhance it if a space serves a function of circulation? How can scale assist in promoting flow? How can scale serve both these concepts?

- The human eye constantly scans its universe, roaming over every surface and void, seeking diversion and entertainment on one level, and meaning and guidance on another. Architects must respond to this seeking on both levels, providing scale-giving features that speak to the underlying human needs.

- The touch, or more precisely the sense that a surface offers potential meaning to the touch, can be a very positive tool in establishing scale. Architects can make use of it by providing surfaces and forms that call out to be touched, stroked, gripped, embraced.

- Light playing over surfaces and voids animates them; and the quality of the light governs the nature and message of their life. The message communicated by the building describes the space, the surfaces, and, most poignantly, the building's scale, our relationship to its physical reality, and our feelings about it.

- While there may be critical social, economic, political, and even moral issues to which architecture must respond, it is not even going to *be* architecture if it does not also respond to issues of scale—issues that touch us individually and as a community by telling us about the quality and certitude of our natural and built environment and about how we fit into the constantly enlarging physical worlds of our existence.

- The concept of completeness, of wholeness, of fitness in design must be observed: even when the parts are all individually present and correct, if balance, priority, and subservience to the whole are lacking, good scale will not be achieved.

- Architects must not seek out or lean on easy formulas of any kind. Uncritical acceptance of a school, a style, a process, a kit of architectural parts signals a failure to use the mind to its fullest capacity and a neglect toward crucial aspects of the designer's responsibility as an architect and as a person serving society.

□ Architects must constantly reach for their greatest potential, must stretch themselves beyond their known abilities, must seek to grow as designers, as anticipators, as human beings, as providers of a better life for mankind.

Let every commission be a quest for excellence, and let excellence ever include scale as an essential component!

Design Credits

- 1-1, 1-2, 3-1, 3-3, 3-16, 5-1, 5-6, 5-8, 5-9, 5-30, 6-1, 6-2, 6-3, 6-4, 6-5, 6-9, 7-17: Edwin A. Keeble
- 1-3, 5-12: MLTW/Turnbull, Frank Orr, Associated Architect
- 1-4: Lon Raby
- 1-5, 8-1: Haury & Smith Contractors (in-house design)
- 2-2, 3-15: William Strictland
- 3-5: Frank Orr/Cain-Schlott Joint Venture Architects
- 3-7, 4-7, 5-26: R. Neil Bass
- 3-8: Warren, Knight & Davis
- 3-14, 7-4: George Waller
- 4-1: Thomas A. Gardner (chapel), Orr/Houk (foreground addition)
- 4-2: Earl Swensson (right; others unknown)
- 4-3, 4-5: Robert Anderson
- 4-4: Taylor & Crabtree (sanctuary), Orr/Houk (foreground addition)

- 4-9: Peter J. Williamson
- 4-11: Sharp & Ittner
- 4-12: Steinbaugh, Harwood & Rogers
- 4-14: Francis H. Kimball
- 4-15, 4-16: Anthemius, Isodorus
- 5-2: Edwards & Hotchkiss
- 5-4, 6-6, 6-7: Thomas & Miller
- 5-6: Earl Swensson
- 5-15: Asmus & Clark
- 5-16, 5-21: Orr/Houk; Edwin A. Keeble, Architectural Consultant
- C-3: Langdon & Wilson, A.I.A.
- C-4: Felipe Toledo Saenz, Ingeniero
- 5-19, 5-33: Burkhalter-Hickerson
- 5-24: Pedro Sylva, sculptor
- 5-25, 7-16: Adolphus Heiman
- 5-31: Thompson, Ventulet & Stainback, with R. Neil Bass
- 5-32: Edwin A. Keeble, with Eggers & Higgins
- 5-35: Pietro Belluschi, Pier Luigi Nervi, and McSweeney, Ryan & Lee
- 6-10: Mitchell Barnett
- 7-2: Ictinus, Callicrates
- 7-11: William Appleton Potter
- 7-12: Robert de Luzerches
- 8-3: Giovanni Pisano (attributed)
- 8-4: Thompson & Zwicker (tower), Edwin A. Keeble (sanctuary)

All others are either by anonymous or unknown designers or by the owners' in-house designers.

Photo Credits

- 1–3, 5–12, 5–16, 5–21: Ed Houk
- 4–15, 5–24, 7–2, 7–10, 7–14, 8–3: unknown
- 7–16: Earle DuRard

All other photographs are by the author. Figures 2–1 and 4–16 were drawn by the author.

Index